THE MAGIC SPARK

Reclaiming the Essence of Who You Really Are

Rodrigo Diaz Mercado

The Magic Spark – Reclaiming the Essence of Who You Really Are
Diaz Mercado, Rodrigo
HappyLivingInstitute.com

Copyright © 2021 Rodrigo Diaz Mercado

ISBN: 978-1-77277-405-4

All rights reserved. No portion of this book may be reproduced mechanically, electronically, or by any other means, including photocopying, without permission of the publisher or author except in the case of brief quotations embodied in critical articles and reviews. It is illegal to copy this book, post it to a website, or distribute it by any other means without permission from the publisher or author.

Limits of Liability and Disclaimer of Warranty
The author and publisher shall not be liable for your misuse of the enclosed material. This book is strictly for informational and educational purposes only.

Warning – Disclaimer
The purpose of this book is to educate and entertain. The author and/or publisher do not guarantee that anyone following these techniques, suggestions, tips, ideas, or strategies will become successful. The author and/or publisher shall have neither liability nor responsibility to anyone with respect to any loss or damage caused, or alleged to be caused, directly or indirectly by the information contained in this book.

Medical Disclaimer
The medical or health information in this book is provided as an information resource only, and is not to be used or relied on for any diagnostic or treatment purposes. This information is not intended to be patient education, does not create any patient-physician relationship, and should not be used as a substitute for professional diagnosis and treatment.

Publisher
10-10-10 Publishing
Markham, ON Canada

Printed in Canada and the United States of America

Table of Contents

Dedication vii
Acknowledgements ix
Foreword xv

Chapter 1 – Real Magic 1
The Magic Spark 7

**Part I: The Eternal Game of Hide-and-Seek,
Lost and Found, Now You See Me, Now You** 13

Chapter 2 – This Game of Hide-and-Seek 17
Hide-and-Seek 19
The "I" in Isolation 22
Think with Your Heart 25

Chapter 3 – Whose Life Are You Living? 29
The Program 30
The Habit of Being Yourself 38
Zombieland 40
Perception 43
Whose Life Are You Living? 48

Part II: Reclaiming the Power of Your Magic Spark 53

Chapter 4: The 5 Things You've Forgotten About Your Magic Spark 59
#1 Divine Source – Your Magic Spark 61
#2 Characteristics of This Divine Source 67
#3 Who Am I? Or Rather, *What Am I?* 73
#4 There Are Two of *You* in There 78
#5 The Meaning of Life 85

Chapter 5: Love vs. Fear 89
The Only Two Energies in This Universe 91
Force – Living in Fear 92
Power – Living in Love 93
Choosing *Power* or *Force* 94
Power vs. Force Chart 95

Chapter 6: Allowing Miracles into Your Life 97
Levels of Consciousness 99
Everything Is Happening at the Same Time 103
Your Attention – Your Superpower 106
A Miracle Requires Faith 109
Spiritual Stewardship 111

Chapter 7: The Gift That Keeps on Giving 115
Your Purpose – The Gift 117
Finding Your Purpose – Finding Your Gift 118
Living on Purpose – Giving Your Gift Away 120
You Are Verb, Not Noun 122

Chapter 8: Manifestation 125
Self-Actualization 127
Choosing Your Reality 128
Your Wonderful Imagination 130
Your Awareness of Being 133
My Manifestation Formula 136

Chapter 9: Living in Abundance 143
Abundance Is All There Is 145
Abundance Is Your Nature 147
Living an Abundant Life 149
Gratitude 3.0 151

Part III: The Way 155

Chapter 10: Reclaiming Your Magic Spark 157
The Pyramids of Life 159
The Pyramid of Destruction 159
The Pyramid of Creation 165
Changing *What Is* 166

Chapter 11: Seven Spiritual Practices to Reclaim Your Magic Spark 173
#1 Abundance 175
#2 Do Less; Be More 177
#3 Mental Diet 182
#4 Listening to the Silence in You 187
#5 Seeing Miracles 189
#6 Stop Feeding the Fire 192
#7 Your True Identity 197

Living From Your Magic Spark 203
About the Author..213

I dedicate this book to you, who is looking for that part of yourself that knows you are meant for so much more; the part of you that calms you when you need it the most, knows that you are not alone, and fuels unconditional love inside of you.

Please know that inside of you, you have all the answers. You cannot be anything less than wholeness, beauty, love, and abundance. Do not let the illusions of the outside world blind you from living your true birthright: abundance, love, happiness, peace, and prosperity.

Acknowledgements

Allison

Muchas gracias for always being my "shining star." You have truly shown me that magic is REAL. You inspire me to be a better version of myself every day. Thank you for loving me the way I've always dreamed true love would be. Thank you for being the kindest and most loving and caring Magic Spark the Universe could have ever put in front of me. Thank you for choosing *love* with me, for giving me the experience of falling in love every day of my life—a true *magical gift*. There are absolutely no words in this entire Universe to describe my feelings for you. I can only hope to show you one day at a time. You are the strongest individual I know—I love YOU.

Perla

Thank you, Mom, for being my #1 mentor, and for being a true example of how important it is to always keep learning. Thank you for your love, your kindness, and your protection. Thank you for the gift of being my mom, for teaching me how to live *magic* in my life. Everything I do is a reflection of who you helped me become. I would have never been able to be where I am without all the guidance, patience, and love you share with me. Thank you for being my star. I feel your love in every breath I take.

Alex

Thank you, Dad, for being my #1 fan, my #1 supporter, and my manager. Thank you for allowing me to see a miraculous transformation of a new YOU. Thank you for spending all that time talking with me, being my best friend, and for being "in spirit" when we share time and space together. Words cannot express the gratitude and love I feel when I think about being your son. I love you; you are my hero. My hope is to be as loving to the world as you have been to me.

Ale

Thank you for playing with me in a field most people may not understand. Thank you for showing me how deep our minds can go, and for allowing me to see more in the invisible world. Thank you for the incredible amount of patience you had when I tried to reach the deep understanding you already had about all of this. Thank you for waiting… Thank you for never giving up on that invisible world I could see before, and thank you for never giving up on who you really are. It took me a long time to come back to that place where you have lived your entire life… But I am here; I am home—I love YOU Ale.

Omar

Thank you for living your Dream Life, for showing me how magic is done, and most importantly, for being the Magic Spark that showed me the book that changed my life. Thank you for being brave, for being loving, and for always having my back. Thank you

Acknowledgements

for sharing with me the "magic sparks" of your beautiful furry family: that all they always did was share their love with me. It is hard to find the right words to express how inspiring it has been to see you transform your life; thank you for simply doing it.

Family

To my grandparents **Rodolfo (Ford), Maria de Jesus (Chuy), Felipe (Pipo) y Estela (Petos): Thank you, I am one with you and you are always with me.**

Gracias tías **Oralia, Alma, Susana, Norma, Marta, Virginia, Bertha, Lupita, Ofelia, Graciela Quirila y Gloria** for being caring, kind, loving and nurturing. Gracias tíos **Rodolfo, Héctor, Raùl, Gilberto GC, Chava, Gilberto F y Avelardo** for being fun, playful, perfect and for giving me the essence of true love. You have been a loving energy in my life. I am blessed to have had the experience of being in your presence, feeling your love. Thank you for gifting me the experience of "family." I was blessed with the best childhood a child can have. Thank you for being the loving, patient teacher you were and you continue to be. Thank you for allowing me to feel love with you.

Gracias primos **Omar, Jessuri, Sandy y Uri** for being adventurous, creative and my mentors in this thing called life. Gracias primos **Enrique, Víctor, Marcos, Marta, Héctor, Maru, Betty, Vero, Laura, Ceci, Mónica, Gilberto y Adriana** for being funny, loud and a true example of love. Thank you for gifting me the lesson of laughter, happiness and joy. You have helped me express who I was meant to be. Thank you for playing with me.

Matt

Thank you for being a true miracle in my life. You gifted me the magic of seeing your transformation. Thank you for remembering your own Magic Spark. Thank you for having your childlike wonder come to play with me. Thank you for being brave an open with me. Thank you for being you – there is so much love inside of you; thank you for sharing that with me.

James

Hermano, gracias for sharing your wisdom, your time, and your love with me. Thank you for always having time to talk and smile. Your FAITH and determination are inspiring; they are pure love. Thank you for sharing your abundance and for showing me how one idea can touch and inspire many lives. Thank you for igniting in me who I am today: I am living and loving my perfect Dream Life.

Louise

Thank you for believing in what we do. Thank you for being a channel of abundance in this world. Thank you, because through your grace and abundance, I have been able to share this content with so many lives. I am very blessed that I met you, and I may say that it was quite magical how you appeared in my life. Thank you for allowing me to get to know you and your family.

Acknowledgements

Christine

Thank you for reigniting your childlike wonder with me. Seeing you transform into a butterfly has been one of the biggest gifts in my lifetime. Thank you for always getting excited about seeing not only magic tricks but REAL magic. Thank you for our friendship; it has continued to blossom into a miracle.

Sathish

Your vision of making things possible has been an inspiration to my life. From not understanding your world to admiring what you do and who you are, has been an incredible gift. Thank you for showing me that living an abundant life, while still playing by your own rules, is possible. Thank you for the love and openness you always have for me.

To YOU

Thank you for trusting me with what I share with you. Thank you for seeing your own perfection, wholeness and greatness reflected in the words I share with you. Thank you for trusting in yourself. Thank you for saying "YES" to you. It is with all my love that I show up in front of you to have a conversation between two Magic Sparks. I learn from you, as much as you do from me. There are no words to express the joy, the peace, the love and the abundance I feel when I see you on the others side looking back at me, as we both learn to Dance with the Divine. Thank you.

Foreword

It has been an honor watching Rodrigo live and love his magic, and become the incredible author, speaker, and emotional & spiritual intelligence GURU that he is today. Helping others truly spark the connection with who they really are.

You are about to enjoy a special treat. This is true *music for your soul* – REAL Magic.

Your Magic Spark, what Rodrigo talks about in this book, is essential to achieving a life of Happiness, Love, Joy, Peace & Abundance.

This book carries incredible wisdom that can help you reach higher levels of consciousness and make a difference in your life – a true transformation from the inside out.

I invite you to open your heart and truly connect with the part of you that knows that you came into this world to experience and share all the blessings and abundance this Universe has for you. Connect with every word in this book, as it has been written with the sole purpose to help you live your best life possible. I can guarantee that if you truly immerse yourself into this wisdom, you will come out a totally different person from the one that opened this book. You will be more and more the REAL You.

This is a true gift for you and *your Magic Spark*. It is my hope that you learn to live from that place that Rodrigo is sharing in this book; that place where all the answers, abundance and love is... yes, all the things you are looking for.

James MacNeil
The REAL Love Guru
International Best-Selling Author and Creator of Pure Spiritual Intelligence

Chapter 1

Real Magic

"If you could simply feel how magnificent you are, if you could fully remember who you really are—or rather what you are—and what it took for you to be right here, right now, all doubt would disappear; fear would fade away. You are Beautiful. You are Perfect. You are Magnificent. You are the entire Universe collapsed in one point in time and space.

You are the reason why the entire cosmos exists. You are the Divine Spark. That is who you really are—real magic. You. Are. Everything."

– Rodrigo Diaz Mercado

In my first book, Sleight of Mind – How to Create & Experience Magic in Your Life," I wrote about how to manifest your desires through your natural state of being of love, happiness, peace, and joy. In that book, I talk about my *awakening* to the concepts from the fields of spirituality, neuroscience, and quantum physics; and how, when combined, those principles and concepts can create *real magic* in your life.

Before writing my first book, I had felt trapped, depressed, alone, stressed, and anxious. I had lost the taste for living. I had asked the big question: ***"Is this (life) really it?"***

My body became sick with three sicknesses, all coming relatively quickly, one after another, culminating with my appendix almost bursting, where I had to be rushed to the hospital to have it taken it out before it was too late.

It was after my appendix surgery that I heard the thought: "Maybe I need to change the way I have been thinking and feeling about life and myself; otherwise, I might not be here (in this life) for too much longer." I cannot tell you where that thought came from, or whose voice I heard that day; but one thing is for sure: **That thought saved my life.**

I now know that that particular thought was the Magic Spark in me. It was the Magic Spark that lives inside of you and me, which *knows* infinite and universal truths about who you and I truly are, and our true, magnificent potential. I want to invite the thought that you are meant for so much more than you are allowing yourself to be right now. I was living like that too; but today, after all that has happened, I am one hundred percent committed to living in my natural state of being of love, happiness, peace, joy, and abundance—our true birthright.

I talk about magic because, in the past, I was a magician. I used to study magic as an art form, had some paid gigs, and had a lot of fun performing magic tricks for friends and family. As a little kid, I always loved magic, and who doesn't? I was in love with the idea of making something that was impossible, possible. I noticed how magic, as an art form, has tons of incredible similarities to the process of how to actually create and allow miracles into your life—REAL MAGIC. Growing up, I thought magic tricks were the only way to experience that sense of awe and childlike wonder; but today, I now know that magic is *real*, and you and I have the power to create it in our lives—it is part of who you and I are.

My purpose, since my awakening, is to do everything I can to prevent anyone from feeling the way I felt back in those dark years of my life. And if you or someone you know might be *there* right now, it's my purpose to help you (or that someone you may know) understand that there is *real magic* all around and inside of you, waiting for you to pay attention to it. It is my purpose to provide the tools, concepts, and practices for you to see your own reflection of true love, your magnificence, and your perfection. You are beautiful and perfect, and you already have inside everything you need to start living a life full of love, happiness, peace, joy, and abundance—your Magic Spark has never left you.

I've been practicing the concepts I speak about in my first book, every day of my life, for the last two years. Since then, I've evolved those concepts and practices; I have been researching and creating new material, and I'm very excited to share it all with you. There is so much to learn, and so much to practice; and my intention is to take deep spiritual and scientific concepts, and translate them in such a simple way that we can all talk about them and understand them in order to change our lives for the better.

My purpose is to share with you how simple it is to live a miraculous life when understanding these simple concepts and principles. It is my purpose for you to start looking at your life as an exciting, joyful, abundant experience/experiment, full of infinite possibilities for you to create real magic (miracles) in your life. Just like in a magic trick, the magic doesn't happen in your hands; it happens in **your mind**. I am simply providing the right environment for you to create the experience of magic for **yourself**.

This book that you are holding in your hands, is a continuation of my work on how to keep creating real magic—miracles—in your life. In this book, I am focusing on my recent discoveries and practices, based on these three lessons:

1. How to **feel** this magic in your life (this is key to manifestation and inner peace)
2. How to **live** an abundant life
2. How to **understand** that you are indeed this *magic* that I talk about

My intention with this book is that you find principles, concepts, and tools to get to your own place of inner peace, to have a better understanding of how important, powerful, and worthy of all the love and abundance you are; and finally, to remember who you really are: a magnificent "miracle," with the birthright of living your *perfect Dream Life*.

The entire Universe is inside of you; you are a holographic expression of the *WHOLE*. Within you, lies the power to live your actual Dream Life. Within you lies the power to create miracles in your life, which I call the *Magic Spark*.

The Magic Spark

"It is important to remember that we all have magic inside us."
– J.K. Rowling

Inside each and every single one of us, there is an invisible force—a mystical, powerful energy—that keeps our bodies alive. It makes our hearts beat, it makes our blood flow, and it makes our brains function—**it orchestrates our entire lives.** This energy, this *spark*, is the same energy that keeps planets *floating,* and the sun hot; it is the same energy that moves a shooting star across the Universe. This spark is a divine gift, and it was placed inside of you to guide you, to power you, and to give you life. This spark is the whole Universe inside of you. This is who you really are: the *Magic Spark*.

The Magic Spark is the invisible part of you that has no shape and no form. It is your awareness of being, your consciousness. It is the piece of you that no one can ever take away from you. It's the part of you that was never born, and it's the part of you that can never die. The Magic Spark is the *real* you. It is always telling you what feels good and what feels bad. It lets you know what your true dreams, passions, and purpose are. It is the voice inside of you that no matter what everyone else says about who they think you should be or what you should do, it guides you to what *you* like, and it shows *you* what you are meant to do.

Perhaps you might have created a habit of not listening to your Magic Spark. Perhaps you have muted it with all the noise from social media, the news, and the busyness that others have created for you. But your Magic Spark is always there; it is your true essence—it is the Universe expressed inside of you.

You were born unique, beautiful, and magnificent. **There is no one else like you; no one can go behind your eyes and see the world the way you see it.** No one could ever have the gift of being you. And I am fully convinced that you *do* know what your Magic Spark is. I am fully convinced that you have felt it at some point in your life, because it is always there, guiding you to find love, to find peace, to find joy—you simply must close your eyes and listen.

Allow yourself to live your life from this Magic Spark; allow it to come forward. Allow it to help you get back to your natural state of being of love, happiness, peace, joy, and abundance. It knows way more than all humanity put together. There are no limits to what you can do when you allow yourself to live your life through your Magic Spark. The Magic Spark is an energy that contains *all possibilities*. It contains all the information you need to live a life full of abundance. It is time to reclaim your Magic Spark and live from this place of love, light, and abundance.

Funny enough, when you were a kid, you lived from this place—from your Magic Spark—and you totally knew that magic was *real*. Simply take a look at any kid "being a kid"; they know how to manifest love, happiness, peace, joy, and abundance into their lives. They live the *secret formula of manifestation,* which we as adults really crave to know or understand. The answers are simpler than you think; it is **the practice** that brings magic back into your life. And perhaps the word *practice* is not the right word to use. Maybe a more clear and all-encompassing word would be the word *playing*. Just like a kid, you are meant to keep *playing*.

When you are playful—similar to when a kid is playing—there is no right or wrong, or winning or losing. There is just enjoying; there is just playing in the *now*—there is no attachment to the outcome. And it is only in that energy of playfulness that miracles can happen. *When did you let your life get so serious?*

Throughout this book, I will help you get back in touch with that Magic Spark by sharing concepts from the fields of spirituality, neuroscience, and quantum physics. I mention spirituality, neuroscience, and quantum physics because, whether you are aware of it or not, and whether you like it or not, all life is affected by these three fields. I believe it is so much better for me to *know the truth,* so that I can at least make the choice of what to create in my life, rather than feeling like the victim of it. But please don't get too hung up on those terms (spirituality, neuroscience, and quantum physics), as I will do my best to explain that these principles and concepts are: (1) very simple, (2) present in your everyday life, and (3) when practiced, they will create real magic—miracles—in your own life. It was only through simplicity that I was able to transform my life and start living my Dream Life; and it is my purpose to do the same for you.

This entire book will take you through the journey of becoming more familiar with that *Magic Spark* inside of you. This book is separated into three parts:

Part 1

In Part 1, I talk about the reasons and understanding as to why 95% of the world is not living a fulfilling life. (Yes, there is a reason, and it is time to understand and study it so that you can become free of it.) The purpose of Part 1 is to help you realize that up until now, you may have not used that *Magic Spark* to create the life you wish to live; rather, you have used that *infinite power* to create a life that you were told to create, a life you might not be completely happy or at peace with.

Part 1 explores concepts to help you become more aware of what I call *The Program*: a series of ideas, beliefs, and limiting conditioning that have been implanted in our brains through structural behavior throughout entire generations. *The Program* concept is key to understand, as this is the first step to liberate yourself to be able to reach your full potential, your *Dream Life*.

Part 1 is the foundation to "waking up" and understanding how to transcend what has been holding you down and preventing you from living your birthright—a life full of love, happiness, peace, joy, and abundance.

Part 2

In Part 2, I talk about key concepts that you and I have forgotten along the way. These concepts are based on the laws of the Universe, those kinds of laws that are always present and influence everyone's lives, whether we are aware of it or not, and whether we like it or not. These concepts, based on universal laws, are metaphysical concepts—concepts beyond the physical—that are based on the fact that everything in this Universe is made up of energy, and that life (this energy) is being "glued together through a *unifying field*," be it called Divine Intelligence, the Universe, Source, Love, God, etc.

Part 2 talks about all the lessons, concepts, and principles that I wish I had been taught in school: principles, concepts, and teachings on how to achieve inner peace, manifestation, and a life full of abundance.

Part 3

Part 3 of this book is the practice; it is the rewiring of the brain. It is the "how" in *"How* can I change my life?" I have been practicing and learning and creating these concepts, techniques, and meditations (imagination processes) to share with you in order to transform your life. It is with all my love that I share with you here, everything that has helped me completely change my life and live a life full of abundance. I am confident that what is in this book will bring a sense of love, happiness, peace, joy, and abundance into your life.

If I've done my job correctly, the material presented in this book will seem new to you in some ways, yet something deep inside of you—that Magic Spark—will recognize that you already knew all of what I am sharing here. It's my hope that through the words and concepts written in this book, you are able to reflect your own magnificence, greatness, and perfection. Because I am a true believer that I am not able to teach *you* anything, what is really happening is that you are reflecting your own greatness in the words you are reading on this page. It is not me that is creating *magic* for you; it is absolutely one-hundred-percent *YOU* that is creating *real magic* in your life.

Please know that you are already worthy of *all* the well-being, and *all* the love and abundance that this beautiful life has to offer. As I mentioned before, it is your birthright; you must simply remember to stop and be *who you are meant to be*. This is what this book is about: Stop the busyness and remember your true self—the Magic Spark.

Part I

The Eternal Game of Hide-and-Seek, Lost and Found, Now You See Me, Now You...

Part I

The Eternal Game:
Hide-and-Seek
Lost and Found,
Now You See Me,
Now You Don't

"The best way to find yourself is to lose yourself in the service of others."

– Mahatma Gandhi

Chapter 2

This Game of Hide-and-Seek

Hide-and-Seek

Throughout the 1950s and 1960s, there was a British writer and speaker named Alan Watts, known for interpreting and popularizing Buddhism, Taoism, and Hinduism for the Western audience. His teachings live beyond his time and are quite eye opening.

In one of his analogies, he talks about this beautiful metaphor between you (the identity you have of yourself) and your highest self (who you really are: your divine self, the Magic Spark I talk about). This metaphor talks about the children's game, Hide-and-Seek; but in this metaphor, this game is played between you and your highest self:

"God also likes to play hide-and-seek, but because there is nothing outside God, he has no one but himself to play with. But he gets over this difficulty by pretending that he is not himself. This is his way of hiding from himself. He pretends that he is you and I and all the people in the world, all the animals, all the plants, all the rocks, and all the stars. In this way, he has strange and wonderful adventures."
– Alan Watts

Understanding this metaphor is such an eye opener. What this means to me is that there are two of *you* inside of *you* playing this game! The first one is your ego—a false identity of yourself—an idea of who you think you are through your name, nationality, gender, job title, etc. And the second one is your True Self, the

The Magic Spark

Divine Intelligence that you are, that Magic Spark—the invisible part of you that has no name and no form—the part of you that is unlimited.

It makes so much sense to think that *this* is what's happening inside of you and me all the time. Do you ever have days where you feel so inspired and in love with life? You feel like everything is going perfect. You feel unstoppable and you feel in flow. You feel like you are worthy of all the beauty this world has to offer. Well, you feel this way when your highest Self, your True Self, is the one playing this game of life. The truth is that this *Self* is your natural state of being, and here you will always feel love, happiness, peace, joy, and abundance. This is your Magic Spark. You feel loved, you feel powerful, and you feel on purpose—this is the *real you.*

On the contrary, have you had days, weeks, or perhaps even months or years, where you have felt like nothing is going your way? You feel trapped, and you feel sad, depressed, anxious, stressed, etc. No matter how hard you try, things do not seem to go your way. And all of a sudden you wonder: "Where did all that *goodness* go?" Well, this is your ego at play. This is not the real you; it is a *mask* that has now taken over and is now playing this game of life in your place. If you are using the mask of ego, you will always feel trapped, jealous, angry, sad, unjust, in lack, not worthy, alone, etc.

When you look at it this way, life becomes a true game of hide-and-seek, where your Highest Self slips away from you, runs away, and hides in the problems or situations of life, until you look within and find it again—you find *inner peace.* You're always playing a

This Game of Hide-and-Seek

game, and this game might have other names, like "Lost and Found" (feeling lost and then finding your inner peace); or even like in magic, *"Now You See Me* (your highest self) *and Now You Don't"* (*it* is gone and now all you see is ego). But you are always playing this game between yourself (ego) and your "Self" (Highest Self).

From this point of view, you now understand that whenever you are feeling bad, it will eventually go away (as it is all a game)—but yes, you do need to *seek* your Highest Self from time to time. You do need to find that invisible part of you that brings *wholeness* and *peace* into your life, and the search is within. So do not get impatient with yourself when you are feeling frustration and desperation; it is only the ego playing the game. If you feel any negative emotion, simply stop, and seek within. It happens all the time; it is an eternal game—simply be aware of it.

I want to share with you that the most interesting thing about my experience with this hide-and-seek game, is that it helped me write this book. I got inspired to write this book after a couple of weeks where I had not felt like myself. I had just experienced two weeks where I couldn't understand why I was feeling the way I was. My mind had been occupied by negative thoughts. My body had been filled up with negative emotions such as fear, frustration, anxiety, and stress, amongst others. I then understood that my Highest Self had gone *hiding,* and it was time for my awareness to do the internal *seeking.* And if this is happening to you, please remember this:

Every time you are feeling like something negative in your life is happening around you, you might be playing this game of

life through the ego self; as your Highest Self—the real you—could only be experiencing your natural birthright of love, happiness, peace, joy, and abundance. Even in what could appear to seem hard and terrible, your Highest Self will only see goodness.

The "I" in Isolation

This book was written during a time when the entire world stopped; life completely changed as we knew it. This book was written in a time when I personally needed to remember the lessons, steps, and teachings of love. Fear and stress had taken over people. Everyone in the entire world had been asked not to leave their homes for an indefinite period of time, as a pandemic virus had been spreading around the world uncontrollably. The only way to prevent more of its spreading was to stay inside our homes.

Even though, in the beginning of this, fear had taken over a lot of people, fear had not come into my life. I had not given attention to any of the thoughts I knew could start causing fear. After one week of being at home, I felt fear. Even though I was not paying attention to the news or to anything in social media, I began to feel fear out of the blue; I wasn't focused on feeling good anymore. An old back injury had come back. (I believe there are no coincidences. My body started to reflect my way of thinking and feeling.) I was also laid off (a lot of people lost their jobs at this time, and a survival fear took over a lot of people), and no one was hiring. I felt like my world had crumbled in the snap of the fingers.

This Game of Hide-and-Seek

The first few days, I couldn't get over that feeling of fear. I felt frustrated because I had been practicing how to be a peaceful, spiritual person and teacher for over a year and a half; and here I was, feeling fear, stress, and anxiety. But then I had a thought, a miracle... "Rodrigo, you are judging yourself." This was a miracle, because as soon as I realized I was giving myself a hard time for the thoughts and feelings I was having, I was able to separate myself from "the body," from "the thoughts," and from "the feelings."

I was able to realize that I am not any of those things (body, thoughts, or feelings). I am but the one who experiences those things. I am the awareness that experiences the thoughts, feelings, and actions. I cannot be anything that I am aware of, as when I become aware of *anything*, that which I am aware of becomes the object, meaning I must be the observer of what I'm observing. And the same applies to you. You don't confuse yourself to be your cellphone, because you are aware and can observe that your cellphone is over *there* and not *here*.

A year and a half ago, I wrote my first book: *Sleight of Mind – How to Create & Experience Magic in Your Life*. It is a book where I talk about how you already have everything you need to start living your Dream Life. It is the story of how I went from a dark place of sickness, anxiety, and sadness, to living my Dream Life. It is a book on how I broke the habit of being myself, and transformed my old self into a new self. In my book, I give thorough ideas and concepts on how you can start creating magic in your own life. Yep, I used magic as a metaphor for miracles, as I am also a magician. I've been performing magic tricks for about 10 years now. I love the feeling of how something impossible becomes possible, even for just a few seconds.

I went back to digging deep and going within. After all, we had been asked to "stay home" to avoid spreading the virus. The message was clear: *"Stay inside your home,"* which, to me, translated to, *"Go within "my home" ("myself")*. At the beginning, it was not a comfortable thing to do, and it was a little bit scary as well, as I had convinced myself that I had overcome a lot of the things of my past (past bad habits). But as I am learning in this journey, the ego (the self-sabotager) is always looking for an opportunity to bring the worst out in oneself—in my case, this happened after my wife was also laid off from her job, and then our two incomes had disappeared.

I am so grateful that I had to go through this again. I was given a very humbling experience, where I had to accept what was happening (fear, frustration, and anxiety) and simply allow my inner wisdom to guide me to remembering the truth about myself—the same truth I want you to rediscover.

After going through this process of finding inner peace, I felt that there was another book in me. Right now, as I am sitting in my home office during this unprecedented time, I am simply allowing spirit into this paper.

This is a book to help you recover your way into your natural state of being of love, happiness, peace, and joy. This book is a manifestation of the lessons I put into practice, not only whenever I become misaligned with who I truly am, but also every day of my life. This book is an expression of love, happiness, peace, and joy. It is a "knowing," which I am simply allowing into paper. It is divine wisdom, which you and I already have within but might have forgotten along the way.

My intention is for you to read this book whenever you need a reminder that love, happiness, peace, and joy are natural; they live inside of you and they are always with you. It is simply a matter of allowing them to come from inside of you—they are your birthright. It is my intention to put these concepts in a way that helps you get rid of, or notice, belief patterns that might not be helping you anymore; thoughts and feelings that might be causing fear and stress in your life. I know I needed this book. I needed to remember the teachings, the lessons, the love—"the way." It is my intention, in a simple yet powerful way, to help anyone looking for that way back into finding inner peace—that Magic Spark.

Think with Your Heart

I want to share something with you that happened to me in the beginning while studying concepts from the field of spirituality. In the beginning, I found myself over-analyzing everything; I found myself trying to rationalize every single detail I was learning. And it finally hit me: "I must stop myself from analyzing every single detail because, in the past, I have categorized myself to be *a rationally-oriented* person." I ask you to please stop doing the same. I am asking you to please be open and understand the following.

The Magic Spark

I am sure you understand the concept of duality in this world: yin and yang, day and night, light and dark, good and bad, etc. The brain also experiences duality, as it is divided into two: the left and the right side of the brain. By the mere nature of this organ, which is divided into two, you will always have a sense of duality, an internal back and forward.

So when you read something that is very profound, something that could deepen your understanding and relationship with this Divine Intelligence and this invisible world of energy, your brain, by its own nature of being divided into two (duality), will present some kind of resistance. This is why it is very important to **think with the heart,** or rather *feel* these concepts.

The heart, on the contrary, does not experience duality, and this is a fascinating discovery. The heart is one **whole** organ. Its nature is **wholeness**—there is no duality. The heart is the center of life. It is where you feel the most powerful emotion: love. The heart understands universal truths that transcend time and space, and therefore it also transcends the understanding of the brain. I am very confident to say that if you allow yourself to *think* with your heart, all the divine, spiritual concepts you might read or study will be perfectly understood at the heart's level. This is why, in the wisdom literature, it highlights that:

*"Above all else, guard your heart,
for everything you do flows from it."*
– Proverbs 4:23

This Game of Hide-and-Seek

You might not **fully** understand all spiritual concepts that you might read or study right now. It might still take you a little bit of time to come around to some of them, but at some deeper level, you will feel peace and love, even if you have no idea (at an analytical level) what you are reading. When this happens, a part of you has connected with the Divine Intelligence in you—that Magic Spark. Your heart is the gateway to understanding who you truly are, your connection to your Source, and that there are no limits to what you can do. The *Magic Spark* is inside your heart; it is the center of your Universe.

Your heart is actually one of the steps inside my 5-step formula on how to create magic in your life." Inside my workshops, I share the deep meaning of the role your feelings play in creating the life you are currently experiencing, and the one you want to live. Your heart (your emotions) is such a key component in how to live a life full of abundance and happiness.

Chapter 3

Whose Life Are You Living?

The Program

"Some people die at 25 and aren't buried until 75."
– Benjamin Franklin

Have you ever felt like there is more to life? Have you ever asked yourself:

"Is this it? This cycle of waking up, rushing to work to get rushed to work, to then rush to pay bills, to then rush to get home, to rush and go to bed, so you can rush to wake up and do it all over again? Is this really it?"

I know I did... But what about the things you like; what about the things that inspire you?

My realization about this "Program" concept that you are about to read, happened about three years ago. Understanding what "The Program" is, was a complete eye opener and tipping point in my life. All of a sudden, I understood all the reasons why I had felt depressed, trapped, and anxious all this time. I understood that perhaps I hadn't been living my own life, and that I had been living someone else's idea of "life."

After realizing what "The Program" is, I was born again. Since then, I am committed to my happiness, to being aligned with **abundance**; I am committed to living my Dream Life—and how could I not be? I know too much now. I can't unsee what I've seen. And because of this, I am committed to help you and everyone else never feel the way I did: that you're not enough, that life is against you, that you're not lovable, or that you're not capable of. YOU are perfect in every way. You are a "blessed blessing," as my friend James MacNeil says. Love and abundance are your birthright. And today, I am committed to help you reconnect to your true essence: your Magic Spark.

When this whole pandemic-isolation thing happened, and everyone was sent home for an unknown period of time, I realized that once again I had lost my grip and understanding of "The Program" concept. I had become "sloppy" in my thinking, and had let this "Program" overcome some of the work I had already been doing. And it was only then that I became aware that what you're about to read is a constant learning experience. I understood that you never "get there"—life is a constant evolution of the self and awareness.

Understanding The Program will liberate you as well, and allow your Dream Life to start coming into your experience. You will feel inspired to allow the right resources, people, and circumstances into your life, and inspire love, happiness, peace, and joy in how you choose to live moving forward.

The first part of the book is to help you in your personal understanding of why you might feel stuck, stressed, unhappy, anxious, angry, etc. You might already be familiar with this concept, or perhaps this might be your first time hearing about it. But wherever I find you in this journey, my hope is for you to remember that **you** are the one who has the power to create your reality, and the first step is to shine light on what's not working. The first step is to awaken your awareness and become the scientist of your own

Whose Life Are You Living?

---

life. The first step to change is to accept *what is*.

So, What's the Program?

When you came into this world, you were **explained** what money, love, work, and abundance (if you were lucky enough to hear that word around you) are. More than *explained,* you were *passed on* limited perceptions and beliefs on these subjects from those around you. You were pretty much given an already-chewed piece of chewing gum. What you today know to be *true* was explained to you by your parents, uncles, aunts, grandparents, friends, social groups, etc.

Most people, me included, learned a totally ***limiting belief system*** when we were just kids—the information shared went straight into the subconscious mind, our hard drive. Everything you know about ***money, work, love, abundance, etc.,*** you learned based on these three things:

1. **What you were told** (what your parents and your social circle told you that "life" is)
2. **What you saw** (how you saw your parents and others interact with money for example)
3. **What you experienced** (what you first experienced on a specific subject)

For example:

You were told, you saw, and you experienced that going to school, going to college and/or university, getting a job (which you have to hold for 35 years), getting married, buying a house, having a family, retiring at 70, then dying around 85, was called *life*... Well, I am here to tell you that **it is not**—that is a total lie—and you, blindly believing that, is what is called ***The Program.***

What you just read in the paragraph above, is a simplification of "The Program." Essentially, "The Program" is a cookie cutter set of limiting thoughts, feelings, beliefs, and behaviors that have been passed from generation to generation onto you and me. This "Program" goes beyond what I've just described in the condensed version above. It goes really deep; so deep that it already is so ingrained into your brain, that you might have some resistance to noticing it or even seeing it in the very beginning.

There might be some resistance coming up as you read the following statements, and you might find yourself asking yourself questions or making comments such as, "Well, that's how life is *supposed* to be," or "How else am I supposed to achieve my dreams?" Or, "Of course success is achieved by working hard (is it really?)," or "But real life is like this," etc. If there is some resistance in you, this is good. It simply means you are hitting the right button, and your ego is trying to hide the truth from you. For now, flow with it; be open to the possibility that life might not be what you have thought of it (or what you have been told). And please do not feel bad, but instead feel liberated; feel free! Answers are coming.

"The Program" goes deep. And I will do my best to describe it to the best of my abilities today.

Whose Life Are You Living?

Perhaps you have heard, or you have been told, one or a bunch of the following statements (I am confident that there are still hundreds of thousands of statements that I am missing on this list and/or are not aware of yet):

- You need to do something to obtain something.
- You need to work hard in order to make money and be successful.
- Life is hard.
- Some people are just lucky.
- Good things are not supposed to be easy.
- There is not enough time during the day.
- Life is not a fairy tale.
- Imagination is just for children.
- Nice girls don't act like boys.
- People are selfish.
- Life is out to get you.
- You are not lucky.
- Miracles are not a real thing.
- Failure is necessary.
- There is not enough energy to accomplish it all.
- Stop being playful and get serious.
- You must get a job; it is what's normal.
- Money doesn't grow on trees.
- Boys don't cry. Boys shouldn't be oversensitive.
- Money is the root of all evil. Rich people are evil. Money will make you evil.
- Big amounts of money are hard to get.
- There's not enough for everyone.
- Stop doing what you love; get a real job.

The Magic Spark

- A job is just a job, and it shouldn't be fun.
- Money creates problems.
- You must suffer before getting rewarded.
- You must have a house. You must get married. You must have a family.
- That's how life is supposed to be (hurtful, hectic, and sucky).
- True love is hard to find.
- Etc.

I could go on and on here, but my primary purpose is for you to notice that perhaps **you have been living a life that you have not even chosen, up until this point.** You have picked along the way what is called "The Program," a collective set of ideas; thoughts of how people think life *should be*. Perhaps you learned some of these things from your parents, others from your friends, and others from your teachers and colleagues, but you cannot judge anyone else, as it is also not their fault. They were simply passing on what was passed on to them as well. They were simply living their life through this computer "program" as well.

"The Program" might be very hard to see in the beginning, and unfortunately, 80% of people in this world will live their entire lives not being aware of it, going through life without dreams, bouncing from one place to another, just like a zombie. But once **you** see this program, it is so obvious, and you cannot go back. Please take a moment to re-read the quote at the beginning of the chapter and see the incredible meaning behind it, now that you understand "The Program."

Whose Life Are You Living?

Ask yourself this question: Where did all of my beliefs come from? The answer: not from you. They were drilled into you; you learned them, believed in them, and accepted them as truth (your reality). And how could you not? You were just a child. There are so many more out there, or I should say "in" there (inside of you). But I simply want you to be aware that life as you know it, does not have to be as limited as you might have been told, learned, or are now experiencing. You are an unlimited spiritual being. You are free to create your own reality, which we'll get more into, in the following chapters of the book.

Living inside "The Program" was the reason I felt sad, angry, lost, trapped, and even depressed. And this might be happening to you as well. But I can now see that depression is not a negative experience at all:

Depression is simply your body saying:
"Screw you! I DON'T like the person you have chosen to be.
Please try something new. Keep looking; there is more
to life than what you have chosen to be at the moment.
Listen to your true desires."
– Rodrigo Diaz Mercado

If you at any point have felt sad, trapped, angry, lost, or depressed, please be kind to yourself. I know that when I felt these feelings, it took me a couple of years to realize what was happening. I didn't know that my body was trying to tell me this message, but I do now. And I am here to tell you that the only reason those feelings are present in your life are for you to surrender to the fact that there's an invisible part inside of you—your Magic Spark—which knows that there is a lot more out there for you.

There is a beautiful, magnificent, fulfilling life that you are meant to live, and it is just waiting for you to pay attention to it—it is as simple as that. Your Magic Spark is simply hinting at you that changes have to start within. It is telling you that this model of "The Program" you have been trying to follow, in fact, is a total lie.

Life is easy. Life is effortless. Life is beautiful. Life is kind. Life is loving. You deserve all the love, happiness, and abundance in this Universe by the mere fact that you exist. The simple fact that you are alive right here, right now, means you have a purpose. There are no mistakes in creation. And your purpose is to live your best possible life. There are ZERO mistakes in creation.

"If GOD puts this much detail into every snowflake, what makes you think your life is any less important?"
– Unknown

The Habit of Being Yourself

In my book, *Sleight of Mind – How to Create & Experience Magic in Your Life*, I talked about how YOU are a habit. I mentioned that you **are not** your name, you **are not** your nationality, you **are not** your gender, you **are not** your age, and you **are not** your job title or what you do. In other words, you are not what you are currently identifying yourself with. These are all ideas that you have of yourself that you keep repeating over and over again; therefore, you truly are convinced that you are all of these. And the biggest shock is that you didn't even choose any of those things.

I also talk about how even feelings are habits. Ask yourself: "What are the feelings I tend to feel most of the day?" If the answer is stress, anxiety, rushed, anger, depression, guilt, etc., you have trained your body to feel these feelings most of the time. You have created those habits. I am not saying this to make you feel any guilt or to make you feel bad. This is an empowering realization to become aware that if you have maybe created the habit of not feeling good, you can create the habit of feeling bliss, love, peace, joy, abundance, health, etc. Your life is in your hands, and that is freedom in itself. You are not the victim of any circumstance, and we will talk about all of this as we get into the book.

A habit is an automatic, unconscious thought, behavior, and emotion, acquired through repetition. The keyword here is "repetition." So why am I saying this? For the entire length of your life, you have repeated inside your head, and to others, that you are your name, gender, nationality, and age, and that your personality is a certain way; and now, you are defining yourself through thought alone. You are defining yourself by ideas of your past. Therefore, you are creating the habit of being an idea.

What I am trying to say is that throughout "The Program," you have created an avatar—a fake identification of self. And this "avatar" is the one living your life. You have given your power to an idea, because as we will get into in the following chapter, you are none of those things; you are not the avatar. You are Source Energy, manifested in a human body. You are Divine Intelligence, living in a case you call your body. You are pure energy. And understand that this is how you can get out of "The Program" and allow what has always been your birthright: love, happiness, peace, joy, and abundance.

But first, let's take a look at how "The Program" creates zombies!

Zombieland

You just read about "The Program"—that cookie cutter set of thoughts, feelings, beliefs, and behaviors about how life *should be* according to others, which have been passed from generation to generation. And the most interesting part of understanding "The Program," is that "The Program" creates zombies…

In his Pure Spiritual Intelligence metaphysical success philosophy, my friend, James MacNeil, has an insightful point of view on how people love zombie and apocalyptic movies. The reason is that the zombie apocalypse has already happened, and it is still happening right now, every day in our cities. Simply turn around and look on any street, any bus, any subway car, any car, or any office in the city. You will see multiple zombies (the walking dead) looking down at a screen, going from one place to another, without living life. Just like a zombie, it seems that people have lost their ability to live, to connect, to enjoy. It seems like they are not quite alive, but they are not quite dead either.

Whose Life Are You Living?

To be completely honest with you, I was one of them about 3 years ago.

An honest question to ask yourself is: "Is this happening to me?" (With all the love in my heart, I can confidently tell you that "yes," this is happening to you, at some level, shape, or form.)

As a matter of fact, this *zombie mode* is not something that goes away completely, unless you learn how to be present every second of every day. For example, let's say you have been practicing meditation; you are feeling really good about your connection to Source, and you have also changed the way you look at life. But all of a sudden, you get an email from work, on Sunday at 10 a.m., telling you that you need to drop your Sunday plans and head to the office to take care of some "urgent" matters. You all of a sudden jump into a state of anger, stress, and anxiety. You find yourself expressing that your boss is unjust, selfish, and that you hate your job and that your life is now ruined (or at least your Sunday). You arrive at work and take care of the "urgent matter." You return home, and now it is 6 p.m. The entire day is ruined, and you are in a bad mood. You decide that after dinner you will relax and try to forget about the issue… Let me tell you that from 10 a.m. (when you got the email) up until 6 p.m. (after you came home to relax), **you were a zombie. The second you jump out of your natural state of being—of love, happiness, peace, and joy—you are now in** *zombie-mode.* You are not living your true purpose; you are feeling emotions that "The Program" told you to feel when your boss tells you to work on a free day.

Please remember that you are not reading this book to judge yourself; I am not writing this so that you can feel bad about it. I am showing you the tools and concepts that helped me "wake up" and make a conscious commitment to myself **to no longer be a victim of my own limiting beliefs, and to no longer feel like I am not in control.** I am committed to **live my best possible life, and completely and truly understand and align with the fact that love lives inside of me, is who I am, and is who you are too.**

Please remember that the way most people are living their lives is a behavioral pattern—a habit, a cycle—that was learnt through accepting someone else's (a collective consciousness) limiting idea of what "life is." It doesn't mean it is the truth, and this is for sure happening to you at some level, as it is still happening to me at some level. But don't worry; we will continue to rediscover, throughout this book, that you came from a Divine Source, and that same Divine Source is still within you—it is you! Everything else that you have identified yourself with, like your name, nationality, gender, profession, age, and other multiple sets of ideas and/or limiting beliefs, **is not you.** You cannot be anything less than your Source. You cannot be anything other than abundance, love, and power (and you will read and understand all about this later in the book).

"Awareness is freedom."
– **Rodrigo Diaz Mercado**

Perception

"Life is simply an illusion created by your perception —there's nothing else."
– Rodrigo Diaz Mercado

Two people can have a different interpretation of the *same* experience. Here's a good example of this. If you and I were to go to a restaurant, the way you perceive this experience of "the restaurant" will be very different from mine. You might look at the menu, and your perception of the restaurant will be a totally different one than mine, based on what they offer on the menu (as an example). You might look for a salad, and I might look for meat, and maybe someone else looks at the menu and gets upset because they don't offer any vegan options; perhaps someone else looks at the menu and goes directly to the dessert section. There are different perceptions and interpretations of the same experience.

This is fundamental and transformational for anyone to understand, and this alone can and will transform your life—everything you *think/perceive* as the experience of *"your life,"* is purely based on what you have inside, and this means you can only see *out there,* that which you are *inside.* If what you are *inside* is anger, lack, stress, anxiety, and sadness, you will only **perceive** situations and experiences that will perpetuate anger, lack, stress, anxiety, and sadness *out there.*

Here's the thing: the Universe is so generous and wonderful, because it knows that you and I cannot literally see inside of ourselves—you cannot turn your eyes inside to look for what's inside—and because we simply cannot do this, the Universe, with all its generosity and magnificence, simply reflects what's inside of you, using the people and experiences around you. They are simply the mirror of what's inside.

So, for example, let's say you share your Dream Life vision with someone—something you really want to do with your life, like writing books that can help people transform their lives, and from which you can make a healthy living with this passion/calling—and that *someone* says to you: *"I don't believe or think your Dream Life vision is a good idea. The market is oversaturated, and it doesn't seem nice to charge money for helping others in their personal development."* There a few ways you can perceive this scenario (there are many, but here are three very different ones):

You can perceive that this person is against your dream, or that your dream is not good enough, or that you are indeed making a mistake, or that maybe your dream is not the best one, or is really hard to get, or that you might be in the wrong by trying to make a living out of a passion—amongst many other negative things you could potentially reflect into simply words formed by air. And because of this, you might give up and throw your Dream Life vision away.

Or you could understand that you cannot see anything out there in life that is not based on what's inside of you. So if you feel doubt, fear, and unworthiness, this is a reflection that you have doubts, fear, and unworthiness toward your own dream. And instead of getting angry at the person in front of you, you must go within to ask yourself why you are fearful of your own dream, and why it is that *you* do not think that it is natural and OK to make a healthy living from what your true passion and blessing is.

Or (here's a third perception, one that takes a lot of practice and self-awareness) you could understand that what this person is saying to you is his/her own perception and interpretation of what they think life should be. None of what she/he is sharing with you can dictate any of the value toward yourself or your dream. He/she is simply reflecting upon your idea their own fears, doubts, and unworthiness of receiving. On the contrary, if this person celebrates and sees the potential of your sharing, then that's what they perceive to be real for them—that's what's inside.

The moment you realize that you are experiencing only that which you are capable of perceiving, you start to realize that what you perceive as real is not necessarily the entire picture; it is simply what you are capable of seeing at the moment. And in order to be able to see more abundance, love, health, wealth, prosperity, joy, peace, and happiness in your own life, you must change what's inside.

After taking one of my workshops, my clients are realizing how important their perception of what's happening is. They are realizing that what happens is not really that important; the most important thing is their perception of what happens. This is helping them become free!

What you are currently experiencing in your life (the government being wrong, or a particular co-worker being lazy, or that *good* guys do not exist, or that the traffic is what is annoying, etc.), is what your beliefs about life are. If your beliefs about life are that *this* is how life is, then you will find the evidence out there to justify your beliefs. In other words, you will only match your life experience to see and *perceive* the beliefs which you carry inside.

> *"If you think the problem is outside of you...*
> *that's the problem."*
> **– Rodrigo Diaz Mercado**

You must remember that you are the creator of your own life; you are not the victim of what happens—nothing is outside of you. Your perception creates a tunnel vision of life. Because you were raised into "The Program," you have created certain thought patterns and belief systems to tell yourself that life ***is a certain way***, most of which you were actually **instructed and taught** to believe in, meaning they're not even yours, yet you believe them to be true.

There is a *layer* between what happens on the outside (the environment) and what happens on the inside (your understanding of what happens), and that is ***your interpretation of what happens—your perception.***

The outside world simply *is*; there is no positive or negative, no good or bad, and there is no meaning to what happens until you give it one—things simply *are*. At all times, you are reflecting—like a mirror—what you have inside. And if what's inside is anger, injustice, anxiety, stress, and lack, you will only see those same things out in the world; you will align with experiences, people, and circumstances that will perpetuate those beliefs and thoughts you have toward yourself. On the contrary, if what's inside is love, happiness, peace, and abundance, you will only see and align experiences that will reflect the loving, caring, peaceful, and abundant nature of this Universe.

This is pretty fundamental, and I hope that it is starting to make more sense to you: that your perception of things is not necessarily "what is happening"; "what is happening" has *no meaning at all*, and "what is happening" simply *is*. And it is only through your perception of things, that you give "what is happening" some kind of meaning or interpretation. Otherwise, nothing has meaning. You are a meaning-making machine. Your ego feels the need to explain everything; otherwise, the ego feels in danger of dying. (Don't worry; we will talk about the ego conversation later in the book—it's a huge one.)

Understanding this was an eye-opener for me. This means that you have the power to change your perception of things (what's inside), and therefore, your entire life. Yes, it could take time and effort, but this means that your world, as you know it, can completely change to something better—more loving, more peaceful, more secure, more abundant—and overall happier. This is the "how" in "how to start changing your reality through your perception," because:

> *"When you change the way you look at things,*
> *the things you look at change."*
> **– Wayne Dyer**

The Magic Spark

Whose Life Are You Living?

"Whose life are you living?" is a question that is really hard to answer. It requires bravery and true honesty. It requires a deep look at your reality and an honest answer.

I want to ask you: Do you go to work because you want to, or because you *think* this is how life is supposed to be, that this is how money is *earned*, and that this is what you were taught to do since you were a kid (go to school, high school, and college, and get a job)? Have you chosen your career, or is it something that *runs in the family*? Or perhaps you told yourself 20 years ago that *this* is who you are, and now it is too late to change—*what would "they" think*—or that it is impossible to change. Do you always look for the weekend, or for those 2–3 weeks of vacation so that you can rush to a beach and *feel free,* because that is what you are supposed to be working toward?

If most of those questions above made you feel like, *"What else am I supposed to do? This is how life works,"* then you might not be living *your own life*. You might be living *someone else's idea of life*.

As you read in the beginning of this chapter, "The Program" is the cookie-cutter way of living that is taught/transmitted to you—like a virus—in your early years of life. It is the way every person that hasn't seen the pattern thinks and lives. It is how society wants *you* to think; it is how you are trained to think *(you are taught not to ask questions, not to be yourself, to be like everybody else, and to please everyone else in your life but yourself)*. Let me tell you

Whose Life Are You Living?

something that is alarming and requires your whole attention: **"The Program" is meant to kill your Magic Spark.**

For example, inside the current school system:

You are *trained* to raise your hand, to ask for permission to do the most natural thing any living creature does: go to the washroom. You are trained to please an authority figure outside of yourself, rather than to listen to your inner self. You are trained to seek validation from an outside authority.

You are told that asking for help, or looking for an answer from someone else that knows the answer to your problem, is called *cheating* (by the way, asking for help, or seeking the answer to a problem you don't know the answer to, is the most spiritual and natural way of being—a sense of community). You then, later in life, wonder why you have the limiting belief that *you have to do it all by yourself,* or that *asking for help is wrong or a sign of weakness.*

You are told that there is only one right answer to the problem: You either get a check mark, or a red mark for being incorrect. You are trained to believe that there is only one correct way to do things. Yet, today, millions of entrepreneurs have shown that there are millions of different correct ways to do one thing. But most people, because of the "right vs. wrong" limiting belief, live most of their lives saying that *there is only one correct way to success,* and/or they have a very straight opinion on *how you should live your life and do your things,* making you feel that your way is the *wrong* way.

I want to make an emphasis here that I am not talking about the beautiful, loving, and caring teachers, principals, or anyone else that works inside a school. I believe that all of these beautiful souls impart so much love, caring, and kindness into these kids, and therefore into this world. What I am referring to in the paragraph above, is the actual *system* that was created more than 200 years ago and has never been revised. It has never been challenged. I am startled by the fact that we do not teach kids emotional intelligence or spiritual intelligence (not religion), or how to be happy, or how to deal with emotions such as anxiety, depression, or anger, or how to connect with the feelings of gratitude, love, acceptance, and abundance. We do not teach kids how to create wealth and manage their wealth. We do not teach them about self-image, self-confidence, and self-love.

On the other hand, we would rather punish a kid for not knowing how to express him/herself, and for looking for help with a problem they do not know the answer to (cheating)! We give them a judgement through a number—a mark on a test or class—making them feel like they are not worthy of greatness. When getting a low grade or mark, kids don't know that they are not the 50s or 60s on that exam. They haven't developed their self-confidence and self-awareness yet, to understand that this is just a number based on how well they can regurgitate and memorize information. We send a kid to their room or the principal's office for what looks like bad behavior—a *tantrum*—when in reality, the kid doesn't yet have the emotional intelligence to fully express his/her frustration! And the worst is that this happened to me, and this happened to your mom, dad, etc. This happened to you. And this is why I ask the question: *Whose life are you really living?*

Whose Life Are You Living?

I could go on and on with this as a topic that I am passionate about, and this is why, today, it is my purpose to show you that you already have everything you need in order to live a life full of love, joy, peace, abundance, and happiness—you and I simply need to unlearn a lot of what has been passed on to us by accident.

This is the reason why, as a full grown adult, you start saying things such as: "That's not possible," "This is not how things are done," "I have to do things *this* way," "I should...," "I need to...," "I have to...." Or perhaps you always have the feeling that you *need to ask permission for things,* or *you need to please someone else that appears to have authority or power over you.*

The most alarming thing is that this is happening on an unconscious level. Please start to notice if you feel some kind of need to please someone else first, like your parents, your partner, or even your boss. Do you feel the need to ask for permission to do things? Do you feel the need to be validated by others? If you do, for now, have patience and self-love toward yourself, as you were simply trained, just like a dog, to be this way. Throughout this book, you will remember how to live your life through your Magic Spark—the true solution to living a life full of abundance and purpose.

Abundance is real. Abundance is all around us. Stop living a life that is not yours. Do not let anyone else define how you should live your life. You have the answers; the theory is all within. You define your life. It is okay to ask, "Why are things a certain way?" and then do them the opposite way—the way that best fits you.

"If people are not thinking that you are living your life the "wrong way," perhaps you're actually living your life the wrong way."

– Rodrigo Diaz Mercado

Part II

Reclaiming the Power of Your Magic Spark

Once upon a time, there was a baby lioness that got lost. She ended up wandering too far from her family, and ended up lost at a farm full of sheep. These sheep, having such a caring and lovely nature, looked at this baby lioness and decided to raise her as one of their own.

As time passed, this baby lioness learned how to live her life as a sheep: She walked across the valley looking for green grass to eat; she was passive and sedentary; and she even learned how to "baaaaa."

After a few years had passed, something inside this lioness, a voice, was telling her that she was meant for something bigger than just a life behind a farm fence. But when she asked the other sheep why she felt that there was something out there for her, the sheep always responded with the same answer: "You must not know that *this* is how things *are* and always have been; *this* is who you are (a sheep). *This* is what's normal, and *this* is what you are supposed to do."

One day, a young lion came to the farm and was very confused when he saw this particular lioness having the life of a sheep. He decided to convince the lioness to come with him in order to show her what her true nature was.

The lion took the lioness back into the jungle, where the lioness saw other lions for the first time in her life (as she didn't remember where she had come from). The lion took the time to show the lioness around but also what it meant to be a *lion*.

The Magic Spark

"Look," he said. "You are a lion, and lions are kings and queens. You are divine by birthright. You are a powerful, magnificent, and an incredible creature, worthy of all the abundance this life has to offer. Simply listen to your inner voice and let it tell you who you truly are."

The lion asked the lioness to roar, but when the lioness tried to roar, at the beginning, she could only "baaaaa" (just like a sheep). It took her a bunch of tries, but finally, one day, the most beautiful and powerful roar came from deep inside her soul, and the whole earth rumbled. She knew she had been waiting for this feeling for her entire life. It felt like the most natural thing, and she felt worthy of freedom, love, abundance, and all the beautiful experiences life has to offer.

Looking over the valley, the lioness was full of spirit. She was overwhelmed with so much love, happiness, peace, and joy. As she took a deep breath within, and as tears ran down her cheeks, she roared to herself:

> "This is RIGHT!"
> "This is REAL!"
> "This is ME!"

She was home...

The above is one of the most beautiful Sufi Movement stories that I am truly moved and inspired by. It reminds me of my truth and the Magic Spark that lives within me. I hope it also moved you as much as it moved me the first time I read it.

You are the lioness in this story. You and I have been raised to believe that we are something that we are not (a sheep). Please know that you are not your name, nor your age, nor your gender, nor your nationality, nor your job title, nor any of the negative experiences you might have had happen to you in the past, etc.

It is nobody's fault that we were raised this way; everyone else is also trapped in this illusion, "The Program." But for what it is worth, I know that you know and can hear a little voice inside of you—your inner lioness—telling you that there's more to you than what this world has seen, and that there is so much more out there waiting for you to allow it: a world of love, happiness, peace, abundance, and joy. And it is every individual's personal responsibility to wake up and see the truth: that you are worthy of freedom, love, abundance, and all the beautiful experiences life has to offer. This inner roar is that Magic Spark—your divinity.

Chapter 4

The 5 Things You've Forgotten About Your Magic Spark

#1 Divine Source – Your Magic Spark

There is a **Source**, a **Divine Intelligence** that created everything in this physical Universe, including the Universe itself. It exists everywhere (including the spaces you perceive as empty); it is present in everything. It is a God Force that gives life to *all there is*, to both animate and inanimate objects. It is an invisible energy field, that when you slow down your thoughts, It can be felt.

This energy is loving; it is kind, it is beautiful, it is nurturing, it is abundant, it is powerful, and it is unlimited. This Divine Intelligence is what keeps this Universe working in perfect harmony, from all the planets orbiting around the sun, to making your heart beat, as if by magic. This energy is where you and I came from; it is the Magic Spark within. And your connection to *It*, is the most important relationship you can ever develop in this life.

It is not important what we each call this Divine Intelligence; what's important is that we recognize its existence. This Divine Intelligence is always present, whether you know about it or not, whether you recognize it or not, and whether you like it or not.

Different cultures and/or religions have different names for this Divine Intelligence. Even people have different names for *It* as well, so you already might have a name or label you are comfortable with. Here are some of the ones I am most familiar with from our Western Culture: God, the Universe, Source, Allah, Life Force, Source Energy, Divine Intelligence, the Tao (this one comes from the East, meaning "the way"), amongst many others.

It is very important to me to go into a bit of detail about this invisible energy, this Divine Intelligence, this Source, as nearly three years ago, I was completely blind and in denial of it. It is my hope that what I'm about to share with you opens your heart more, to a different and more compassionate understanding of this Invisible Divine Intelligence.

About three years ago, I thought I *understood* the concept that everything around me is made up of energy; but as it turned out, and to be completely honest, I didn't. I have heard phrases such as "We are all one," "We are all connected," "Thoughts are things," and about energy, vibrations, "the Law of Attraction, etc. They all sounded good and pretty. I was convinced I knew what they meant or how they worked—I was a *know-it-all*. But it was not until my *health scare* (my appendix started to burst, close to the time when two other different health problems had been present in my body*)* that I started to really study what this all truly means. I quickly realized the truth: that the more I know, the less I know. I decided to then become a ***not-know-it-all.***

All I ask of you, from now on, is to please be open to reading the concepts on this page. I know there is an invisible part of you, an inner wisdom, that already *knows* the information and concepts of this book—your Magic Spark. I simply ask that you please allow that Divine-Self to come out and play with me for a bit.

Religion –

Not so long ago, I used to have a very strong resistance to the word *religion*. I used to perceive that religions "judge" others that aren't part of a particular group. And even though this might still be happening at some level here and there, I now see the *practicing of any religion* in a very different way. I celebrate that an individual is looking to connect to a source of love; I celebrate the fact that an individual wants to feel love, joy, and peace, because at the end of it all, aren't we all looking to feel this way?

I have simply opened my heart to seeing a different side of it that I have never seen before. I would love for you to be open-minded as you read the following words. I am not trying to change the way you see the world; I am simply presenting a different perspective on things. It is only now that I understand that there are no wrong answers, that if you and I can look at things through the lenses of love and compassion, then it all makes sense.

This next paragraph is only meant to give you a different view from the one you might have had in the past. It is my intention to share the understanding of the power of love and compassion that you can choose at any point in your life, especially when you give yourself the opportunity to let go of what you think you know and what you used to believe in.

The origins of any religion –

Religions were born from people wanting to get to a place of enlightenment and/or peace.

The Magic Spark

For example:

Imagine yourself living 3,000 years ago. Let's say you used to live in a village where there were only 5,000 people. Now, while you were alive, imagine there was this person that lived far away from everyone else in this village. Everyone knew there was something interesting and special about this individual; he/she lived a very peaceful life, and it seemed like he/she knew a different way of living—a more *connected,* happy, all-knowing way of living; a way of living that created abundance and prosperity. He/she was always in a loving, joyful, happy, and peaceful state of being. There was no sign of fear or frustration. And being in the presence of this individual resulted in actually feeling more peace and joy inside of yourself, without knowing why.

Imagine everyone in the village looking at this person and trying to figure out what this person was doing, how she/he was living, or this person's perception of life. So, you and a group of people go out and ask this person about the "hows." Perhaps this individual was willing to share his/her ways, or maybe he/she was not. But regardless of the decision, you decide to observe this person and try to take notes about his/her way of living and his/her teachings.

Your intention, as a village that is studying this individual, is to simply pass on these teachings or observations to better the way you and everyone else live. Your intention is to reach the same level of peace and love that this individual portrays, and help others feel the same way—all you want is for everybody to experience happiness. So, you and others start to try and teach what you have observed. Your intentions are pure, and you are genuinely trying to make everyone's lives better by trying to teach others the way this person was living (at least *your* perception of his/her life).

That is the basis of any religion. And if you are able to grasp that all religions started from a place of **love**, from a place of trying to find the answers to live a better life, to live in peace, compassion, and harmony, then I think you might agree with me to give what religion has become today, a break. We should be more accepting of someone that might have a different vision from ours about a Divine Source. **We are all simply trying our best to connect to something bigger.**

I am not saying that you should or should not practice any religion; I am simply saying that at its pure core, the fundamental teachings of any religion are based on what we are all trying to achieve every day of our lives: love, happiness, peace, and joy. Your life is personal, and your journey is unique, and I know that deep inside of you, you want to feel love, you want to feel peace, you want to feel joy, and you want to feel happiness. I have now become a student of love, happiness, peace, abundance, and joy. And becoming a student of these subjects has allowed me to stop judging anyone's personal path, and celebrate a quest for *happiness.*

Please remember this…

> *"Buddha was not Buddhist. Jesus was not Christian. Muhammad was not Muslim. They were teachers who taught Love…Love was their religion."*
> **– Anonymous**

Understanding this Divine Intelligence –

There is this force that keeps everything together: The sun doesn't explode all of a sudden; the planets don't fall out of orbit; the moon doesn't crash into Earth. The trees keep growing, and the oxygen on this planet is simply here. Everything works the way it should. There is a God Force—a Divine Intelligence—keeping "all there is" together, working in perfect harmony. And the beauty of this is that you and I do not need to do anything at all—it goes far beyond our capabilities.

This same Divine Intelligence exists inside of you, me, and every single living thing on this planet. Think about it: You don't need to keep track of how much oxygen you need to take in every time you breathe; you don't need to worry about how to make your heart beat, or how to make all your organs and systems work together in perfect harmony for you to be alive. This is the Divine Intelligence in you; this is life in you—the Magic Spark.

All the evidence you need in order to understand this energy is to look at what happens when you get a little paper cut on the palm of your hand, or a scratch on your knee from falling down. What happens to that cut after about ten days? Your body, as if by magic, makes that cut disappear—it heals itself. That's the Divine Intelligence in you—the real you. There is something inside of you that wants you to live. There is something inside of you that loves you so much that it makes everything work in perfect harmony, with and without you, and for you. This is life—a God Force inside of you.

#2 Characteristics of This Divine Source

This Love Force has certain characteristics. In his book, *The Power of Intention*, Dr. Wayne Dyer describes 7 characteristics of this God Force (he calls it "Intention"). He describes that this Divine Intelligence is: loving, creative, kind, beautiful, abundant, expanding, and reciprocal. I am going to talk about the characteristics that I've personally found in my own research, and that I have been able to feel with such intensity through connecting back to my Magic Spark.

Your Magic Spark is:

Loving –

How could this God Force, this Divine Intelligence not be loving? It constantly gives life to everything you see. It is constantly nurturing current and new life. It wants *you* and me to live. This Source is always providing a loving energy field. Simply close your eyes and feel *life* inside of you. Feel this loving energy embracing you in the shape of warm and wavy vibrations around you. It makes your bodily functions operate. Love is all there really is in the Universe, and sometimes what might appear as a burden, is 100% a message from "love," asking you to pay attention to what really matters.

Creative –

This Divine Intelligence is creative, meaning it is always in constant creation mode. Creation is its nature. This Divine

Intelligence created and gave life to everything there is. And the most beautiful thing of all is that it never stops creating. It gives life to new things all the time. Once it creates something, it doesn't stop to look at what it created, nor spends time debating if *It* could have done a better job—*It* knows that everything *It* creates is perfect. This Divine Intelligence loves all creations equally, and knows that they are perfect the way they are, so it moves on to the next creation, and the next, and the next...

Beautiful –

Everything created from this energy force is beautiful: the sun, the ocean, the sky, the flower, the butterfly, you, me, etc. Simply look at something, anything; and when you look closely at anything, you can see the perfection in its creation. If you pay close attention, you can see the *whole*—the entire universe—in something small.

Simply try to see beyond the definition, or the connotation that we as humans have given things. Simply look at anything and feel the Divine Intelligence inside of it; feel its perfection—a bird is not a bird when you remove the word *bird* from the equation. A *bird* then turns into 50 trillion cells, unified together by a Divine Intelligence that gives life to this life form that can simply fly across the sky with no effort—pure magic.

I am confident to say that you have felt complete *beauty* at some point in your life. Perhaps it happened when you looked at a sunrise. Or you might have been hiking, or maybe you were at a music performance. Maybe you were watching your kid play or walk for the first time. Maybe it was your puppy. I am very confident when

I say that at some point in your life, you have definitely felt and seen such *beauty* that has inspired an overwhelming sense of *awe* and *beauty* into your life, that tears have run down your cheeks... That is ***true beauty***. And that beauty, the one that feels whole and indescribable, is Source talking to you—it is the Magic Spark in all of us. In that moment, you have allowed yourself to see your Source reflected in this world.

Kind –

Some people tend to believe that we live in a hostile (evil or not fair) Universe. (I used to be one of them. I used to believe that life was not fair or that life was very hard, but now I understand that those were old programs that I had chosen to believe at some point in my life.) And there are some people that *know* that this Universe, this God Force, is benevolent. (I now choose to *know* that this God Force is benevolent and kind.) And how could it not be?!

This God Force, this Divine Intelligence, this Love Energy, is kind. It created life for us. It created everything there is for us to enjoy a beautiful life. This energy makes the sun kindly warm this planet so that we can be the "life" in it. All this Divine Intelligence knows is how to support life, harmony, and love. With an open heart, and simply by looking at nature, you can easily identify how kind this energy is. Look at the sky, look at a flower, look at a bird; all of these emanate kindness.

Abundant –

This energy is abundant, meaning it never ends, it always gives, and it never judges. It is like the sun! The sun never ends; it always gives (light and heat) and never judges. (The sun never says: "You get some light, but you over there don't.)

Abundance is all there is in this Universe. This loving energy never stops giving you what you ask for. It loves you so much that all it does is give you more of what you pay attention to.

Expansive –

This loving energy never stops expanding. Since the Big Bang, the Universe has not stopped expanding; this is why it is called infinite. It has no end, and it is in constant expansion.

Receptive –

This means that this loving energy receives the vibration you are putting out, and reflects this vibration in your life experience. It will give you people, circumstances, or events that have the same or similar vibration to the one you are putting out into the world. This is accomplished through how you feel. Your vibration—which is the language of the Universe–is the way you communicate with this loving energy. So, if you are angry, stressed, and anxious, you are telling this God Force to please send you more people, circumstances, or events to perpetuate more anger, stress, and anxiety. On the contrary, if you are grateful, happy, and in peace, this loving force will present people, circumstances, or events to perpetuate more gratefulness, happiness, and peace in your life. This is the Law of Vibration!

What do these attributes (of this God Force) have to do with YOU?

If I were to ask you to describe yourself... If I were to ask you to please give me a few characteristics of who you are... What would you say about yourself? (Play along, and before you continue to read, answer that question for yourself.) How would you describe yourself?

Did you say anything like tall, short, smart, fit, pudgy, smart, intelligent, not so good with numbers, perfectionist, hardworking, team oriented, analytical, funny, good looking, serious, stressful, relaxed, etc.? Well, I would love for you to become aware that you are describing a personality. And a personality is not what or who you are, these are not your true characteristics. You may have created a habit of believing that who you are is a set of ideas and adjectives that you picked up along the way, or perhaps what others told you that you might be. But I am here to help you understand that this is not true. You have been taught to describe yourself as:

(1) What you see in the mirror.
(2) The labels or ideas you and others have of you.
(3) Your identification with your past.

But none of these three points define your character, characteristics, or your true attributes.

The Magic Spark

Please, you must understand that you are the expression of this God Force, this "energy of love." You are the Universe manifested in a body. You are an expression of life itself; you are the entire Universe collapsed in one point in space and time. And because you came from the same Source that everything else came from, you are a piece of it; **you have the same characteristics**. And this is one of the things you have forgotten along the way.

You are *loving, creative, kind, beautiful, abundant, and an ever-expanding* being. These characteristics are your birthright. They cannot be taken away from you. They are always with you; **they are who you are.** The only reason you might not be able to feel them at all times, is because you might have not allowed yourself to receive and be part of the always-present "flow" of these characteristics. You might have forgotten your true identity, and picked a false self (ego) along the way.

You might have internally blocked this eternal flow of well-being. Right now, you are predominantly choosing to believe and identify yourself with ideas about life or about yourself that are not true (like your name, nationality, gender, age, job titles, etc.). You might have chosen to keep your attention on the labels of your past (the school you went to, the town you were born in, the career choice you made), on thoughts that others have of you, or on your misinterpretation of what you see in your external world.

You have forgotten that your "true self" is a piece of this Divine Source; this is what you truly are—you are 50 trillion cells attached together by the power of love (Divine Intelligence), and that is what you are—the Divine Intelligence "gluing those 50 trillion cells. I

am here to remind you that you could not be anything less than *loving, creative, kind, beautiful, abundant, and ever-expanding; because that is what your Source is.*

Don't worry; as I said before, these characteristics have never left you. They are your birthright. They are always present. And to allow them, you must simply pay attention to them. I will describe the "how" in Part III of this book. For now, I would love for you to start creating the habit of thinking about yourself as *loving, creative, kind, beautiful, abundant, and ever-expanding*. Start by saying out loud to yourself: *"I am a loving, creative, kind, beautiful, abundant, and ever-expanding spiritual being, having a human experience."*

I will now go deeper into the understanding of the concept that you are this Divine Intelligence...

#3 Who Am I? Or Rather, *What Am I?*

"You are not a drop in the ocean.
You are the entire ocean in a drop."
– Rumi

This next section is a reminder of who you are. Here are the strongest concepts, analogies, and "aha" moments that have helped me remember *who I truly am*—but better said, *what I am*.

What you are not –

You are not the body you are looking at. You are not your name. You are not your gender, nor your age, nor your nationality. And you are definitely not the *stories* you keep telling yourself and others that you are.

"**You are not a body that has a soul. You are a soul that has a body.**"

In my previous book, *Sleight of Mind – How to Create & Experience Magic in Your Life*, I went in depth, helping you understand that you are none of those things you have identified yourself with. Those are simply **labels** and **ideas** that you've repeated inside your head, over and over again, and you truly believe that is who you are; it is a habit. Those ideas became habits, and those thoughts became your identity. But I want you to know that that is not who you truly are.

Your body –

How could you be *a body*? It is impossible! The reason why it is impossible for you to be a body, is simply because, every seven years, you are an entirely different body—all the cells that constitute your body have died, and new cells have come to be. **You are the soul inside the body.** And your soul has occupied different bodies by now: It has occupied the body of a 10-year-old, a 20-year-old, a 30-year-old, a 40-year-old, a 50-year-old, a 60-year-old, etc.

When you look in the mirror, you think you are looking at your body. But to be completely honest, you are actually looking at 50 trillion cells all living in a community, all glued together by Divine Intelligence. When I say the word "Rodrigo," I am really referring to a living community of 50 trillion cells, but my ego wants me to believe that "Rodrigo" is one entity, separated from everyone else, and that I am a male, born in Mexico, with X number of years, etc., and that I am not one with my Source, but rather separate from it.

You are not a body; you simply have one. It is a helpful practice to start disassociating yourself with your body. It is very healthy to take the time to understand that you are a walking miracle; you are 50 trillion cells expressing themselves in bones, muscles, blood, organs, etc., all working together in harmony to create this thing you call your functional body. It is a God Force that keeps them working with one another to help your soul to be housed in there.

So, the big question stands: "Who Am I?"

Who you truly are (what you really are) –

A very interesting way to understand what you are, is to look at the question:

"What keeps you standing up?"

When I first asked myself this question, a lot of different thoughts came into my head, trying to answer this from an ego perspective. (I would love for you to think about these questions as well.)

The Magic Spark

First, I said: *"I do."*
Then a voice inside of me said: *"Yes, but what is it that really keeps me standing up?"*

Then I said: *"My muscles and bones."*
Then that same voice said: *"But what keeps my muscles and bones engaged so I can stand up?"*

Then I finally said: *"Aha! My brain! My brain gives the command for me to stand up!"*
Then that same voice, once more, said: *"But who gives the command to the brain?"*

After a little while of going over and over this question, an incredible sense of love and joy came into my body. I felt overwhelmed with happiness as the answer came to me…

"Consciousness, an Infinite Intelligence, a loving God Force (the same God Force that created this Universe). The *thing* that makes me stand up is an incredible energy of love, and without it, life is not possible, because *It* is life itself. *This is who I really am.*"

This is what you really are! You are pure consciousness. You are Infinite Intelligence; you are that God Force. You must be. And the simplest way to understand this is that if you were to die while standing up, that God Force would leave your body (your soul), and your body (who is not really you) would simply collapse to the floor.

Because what was holding it together all along was this Divine Energy. **That is what you truly are.**

Please take a moment to feel that God Force inside of you, that Divine Intelligence that is the real you. I am not talking about your name, your body, your age, your nationality or any *"thing"* you tend to identify yourself with. I am talking about the invisible part of you that shares a connection with everything in this Universe—the same energy that makes a tree grow, a bird fly, and the sun shine. That energy is what keeps you standing up; it is the same energy that keeps your heart beating, your lungs breathing, and your blood running. You are all of it.

Practice paying attention to *feeling* this energy that you cannot see. You can pay attention to it by using your awareness. When you sit in silence (you can also do this while standing up or lying down), feel that invisible part of you, that formless part of you that has no name. When you hit that sweet spot, when you truly start feeling and connecting to it, you will begin to feel peace in your heart. You will start to feel a warm tingly sensation inside and around your body—*welcome home.*

The more you practice this awareness of your True Self, the more you will start to remember who you really are: the entire Universe (life, God Force).

If you feel like this conversation has a lot of depth to it, you are right! Understanding who you really are is something that takes time *to feel.* That is why we go deep into answering the question, "Who Am I?" in my course, Creating Magic in Your Life. It is a beautiful conversation that you and I were really never taught. It is very liberating, and with the correct guidance, it is an empowering truth that sets you free to realize your unlimited potential.

#4 There Are Two of *You* in There

"Your ego is not your amigo."
– James MacNeil

Ego is the shadow inside of you. Where there is light, there will always be a shadow. The ego can never go away, but what you can do is that you can always pay attention to the light, and let the shadow follow, without paying attention to it.

My good friend, James MacNeil, in his Pure Spiritual Intelligence metaphysical philosophy, has the perfect analogy for this...

Do you know what artificial intelligence (A.I.) is?

Artificial intelligence is the creation of a **human-made** machine that is able to think, work, and at some capacity, learn on its own (just like a human).

There are so many Hollywood movies out there, where humans create artificially intelligent machines or robots, and where, after a while, these machines begin to turn against their creators, killing them and almost wiping all humanity away (e.g., Terminator, iRobot, The Matrix, Robocop, amongst others).

The 5 Things You've Forgotten About Your Magic Spark

The reason I bring this up is because your **ego** is an *artificial intelligence*. It was created by you, and it is now trying to eliminate you. Your ego is a *false self.*

Your ego is not real. Ego is simply an idea that took a life of its own. It was created when you were a baby, around the age of two (and it was not your fault). The ego was born simply because, as a baby, you felt separation from love as a consequence of feeling left alone, or hungry or afraid. It is part of our human experience.

The false idea of self (the ego) is so powerful that it is very hard to realize that you are not it. It truly thinks it is you, and you truly think you are it (all of this happened through unconscious programming and limiting beliefs). Your ego defends and truly thinks you are your body, nationality, age, and all the labels that have come to define you.

Ego's only purpose is to eliminate you by making you feel not worthy of receiving love or abundance, by making you feel *less*, guilt, shame, envy, jealousy, not good enough, and especially by making you feel separated from the Source that created you. The ego is that part of you that is always in competition with everyone else. It always wants to "win." It is constantly making you feel like you "need" more and more and more. It wants to compare itself to others and be "better" than the rest. But it is also the self-sabotaging voice that keeps you feeling "less" than everybody else.

Ego creates separation; it creates division, and it categorizes. It wants to separate you from the "whole" (your Source and others). So, when you pay attention to any given *labels*, like your gender,

The Magic Spark

your nationality, your age (depending on how old you are at any given point), the type of family you came from (single-parent, poor, rich, middle-class, no siblings, lots of siblings, etc.), etc., you are paying attention to your ego. You are making a judgement about yourself and others. (This is how you are able to categorize, by making judgements and creating separation.)

Think about it; a nationality is only an idea! Who came up with the idea of countries? A border is an ***imaginary line***—it doesn't exist! The same goes when you think about age, gender, your name, the type of family you come from, etc.; they are all invisible categories and ideas that someone came up with to create labels (judgements).

What you truly are, is a spiritual being living a physical experience. That is who you are. The rest are ideas you have adopted through the *unconscious programming* that has been passed on to you. And right now, it might be really hard to disengage from who you think you are (your labeled identity). But remember that your true characteristics are the same as your Source: *loving, creative, kind, beautiful, abundant, and ever-expanding.* Remember that ego is an artificial intelligence—a false self (an idea) that got really strong.

"Ego's only purpose is to perpetually create fear and separation. It will seek anything from your life experience to make you feel this fear, frustration, and separation."
– **Rodrigo Diaz Mercado**

Here are some examples of how to identify ego's language:

"If I don't get this first, someone else will."
"It is me or you."
"There is not enough for everyone."
"Life is not fair."
"There is good and evil."
"What's the catch here?"
"I am not good enough."
"I am not good at this."
"Things are hard for me."
"Things never work out for me."
"I need to give people a reason for them to love me."
"Why is this happening to me? Life sucks."
"She/he is wrong, and I am right."
"That is not how she/he should do that."
"My answer is the correct one."
"She/he hurt me (she/he did it on purpose)."
"I have experience suffering in my past."

Start a practice where you make a conscious commitment to identify every time ego's voice comes up in your life. When you let your spiritual nature grow, the ego starts to diminish; it loses its power.

Here is how –

Recognize any negative inner conversation that reflects judgement (toward others or toward oneself), fear, loneliness, lack, stress, anxiety, self-sabotage, and anger. Play the game of recognizing that anything that feels negative or unjust in your life comes from ego's voice. The best thing you can do in that moment is to recognize that the voice you are listening to inside of your head is not your true self speaking; it is your ego (your false self). Stare at that thought and say:

"I can see you now. I know you are not my true self. I know what you're trying to do. I acknowledge the *noise* and let it go. I love myself too much to let this thought affect me. I am perfect."

Repeat this phrase as many times as necessary. The intention is for you to start separating yourself from that negative voice (that is not the real You). If you can begin to observe that *fake* voice in your head, you will stop identifying yourself with the emotions that those thoughts make you feel. You will also stop identifying yourself, little by little, with those false statements. Remember, you cannot be anything less than *loving, creative, kind, beautiful, abundant, and ever-expanding*.

What ego wants –

Studying the ego is fascinating. Teachers like Eckhart Tolle, Wayne Dyer, Alan Watts, and James MacNeil have helped me understand the ego in a deeper way. But just when I think I am getting a sense of how to "control" it, it creates more illusions and perceptions to try and create desperation and frustration.

The ego is not real. It is a false self. It is an idea that was born when, as a baby, you began to become aware of "self." In other words, you began to become self-conscious (conscious of self). You began to understand that you had a body and that people had opinions about the way you looked, the way you behaved, and the choices you were making. So, you began to become self-conscious about yourself. Without knowing it, you started to create an idea of who "you were" by defining yourself as separate from everybody else. You started to believe in your name, your gender, and your nationality, and this created a false identity, a false self–ego.

So here are 4 of the characteristics of ego:

Ego wants you to believe that you are what you acquire: your possessions, labels, titles, accomplishments, and failures. It always wants more, and more, and more...

Ego wants you to believe that you are separate from me and everyone else. It wants you to believe that because you have a body, you are separate (not connected) from the world around you. By identifying yourself with your name, nationality, age, gender, job titles, etc., the ego creates the illusion that it is *"you vs. everyone else."* It keeps feeding you ideas such as, "You must compete against others and win; otherwise, you will lose." Or, "Get *X* before someone else gets it," etc. But as you have been reading throughout this book, you cannot be separated from anything, as you are **life** itself *(God Force expressed)*. I am *life* itself *(God Force expressed)*, every animal is *life* itself *(God Force expressed)*, the oceans are *life* itself *(God Force expressed)*—everything is God Force expressed.

The Magic Spark

We are all one; we are all one community of energy that is *life* itself *(God Force expressed)*. Life = God Force expressed.

The ego wants you to believe that you are separate from what your heart desires. It wants you to believe that what you want is over ***there***, and that you are over ***here***. But this God Force (Source Energy) is everywhere—it is *universal*, meaning there's no place where it is not. This means that you are already connected to what you desire. Think about it; everything you desire to experience in your life—wealth, health, abundance, "X" or "Y" experience, etc.—already exists in this physical Universe. It is already here. It is simply not in front of you, but it is already *here*. And this God Force exists in both you and that particular experience or thing that you desire. Therefore, you cannot be separated from your desires, as you both are God Force expressed. In order to pull them into your life experience, you simply align with the vibration of your desires, through the power of your *attention and intention*, by asking yourself: "How would it feel to already have X in my life?"

This one is the most important one that your ego works at... **Your ego wants you to believe (and succeeds most of the time) that you are separate from the Source that created you.** It wants you to believe that you are separate from this God Force, this Divine Intelligence. But this is not possible as you are a piece of this Divine Intelligence; you are *God Force expressed. You are God Force expressed into a human body.* And only because most humans have made the habit of thinking that we are *a body* first, most people have forgotten that we are not a human being having a spiritual experience, but rather we are spiritual beings having a human experience. Here's another way to look at it: If a cat has babies, the cat has baby cats. If a whale has babies, it has baby whales... If Divine Intelligence has babies (everything in this physical Universe), then Divine Intelligence has baby Divine Intelligences...

#5 The Meaning of Life

"You don't have a life. You are life."
– Eckhart Tolle

For the next few paragraphs, I would love for you to have an open mind and, most importantly, an open heart. I ask you to be completely honest with yourself and let these words speak truth to you. I can honestly tell you that I don't know where these next words came from, but every time I read them, an outstanding truth gets shaken inside of me.

One night, I was sitting in my living room talking to my wife, when all of a sudden we started to go back and forth with the following thoughts, which we know came from somewhere else:

- Is it possible that you and I got caught in a mental trap?
- Is it possible that you and I have forgotten what life is all about?
- Is it possible that we have been blinded into living an illusion so powerful that we no longer see the truth; we no longer see our true nature?
- Is it possible that because we are so deep into this illusory way of living that we are actually afraid of going back to remembering that our true state of being is the one of love, happiness, peace, freedom, and joy? This would mean we have

The Magic Spark

played this "game of life" all wrong; and that is very scary. It means that there have been lives that have been lived in complete blindness.

Here is what you think is happening—the **illusion**:

You and I think that because we *exist*, we must *do* (we must always chase after something, or we must always be doing something; what else would we be here for...).

We think that *being* is *doing*.

There is a fear, deep inside of you and me (that comes from the ego), that if we stop chasing after a goal, that if we either stop thinking or stop doing, we might die. You and I think that in stillness, we might die. Ask yourself: "Why do I feel the need to always be doing something? Why do I feel the need to always be thinking about something? Why is there the need of having that little voice inside of me always saying something to me?"

What has happened is that you have actually forgotten that in **stillness,** you *are*.

You have forgotten that inside **stillness** and **silence** resides your true *beingness*, your true *power*.

You have created a habit of feeling that you must "do," and you especially feel that you *must do something in order to get something.*

You blindly believe you must always *be chasing after* something; otherwise, what else would you be here for?

But this is all an illusion, and you and I have been fooled. We have been played by our own ego—the false self—that part of you and I that is not real; that part of you that thinks it is you, but it is not. How could something limited be you? Your nature is unlimited. You came from "unlimitedness."

You have forgotten that your true purpose is **being**, not **doing**.

You have forgotten that the purpose of life is to *live*.

You have forgotten that your purpose as a divine spiritual being is to allow things into existence, by *being*, by inspiration.

You have forgotten that love, peace, and joy are not something you can get (as if they were something you can purchase); *they are states of beingness,* and they are already within you. They are your birthright, and you simply allow them from within.

Creation is finished; you are not creating anything. Everything in this physical Universe has already been created: the wealth, the health, the prosperity, the abundance, the love… Everything that you could possibly desire is already present in this physical Universe—CREATION IS FINISHED! It is now time to enjoy, time to **allow** ourselves to be the things we want to be. It is time to live out what's deeply inside your heart. It is time to **stand still** and simply **be**. Let your uniqueness come out.

The meaning of life is not to ***do***. The meaning of life is to ***be,*** to ***express your Highest Self.*** As Pablo Picasso once said: *"The meaning of life is to find your gift. The purpose of life is to give it away."*

You are not meant to struggle, you are not meant to hustle and hustle, and things are not supposed to be difficult. You are here on purpose, and you can only find that purpose when you allow yourself to ***be***. As I mentioned in my book, *Sleight of Mind – How to Create & Experience Magic in Your Life*:

"Your life's purpose will not come to you through thinking about it, and it will not come to you through your thoughts. Your life's purpose can only be experienced when you live in the present moment, when you are aware, and when you are conscious. It can only be experienced through your heart. It can only be experienced when you are doing what you love; you need to do what inspires you."

This is breaking the illusion.
This is shining light into the shadow.
This is *being*.

Chapter 5

Love vs. Fear

Love vs. Fear

The Only Two Energies in This Universe

In his book, *Power vs Force*, Dr. David R. Hawkins describes how there are two energies in this physical Universe: Power and Force. And you are always living your life from either one of them at all times.

The energy of *Power* is an energy that is caring, loving, and nurturing, and it gives *you* energy. Most importantly, as you will read in the next pages, *Power* also has to do with how easily things flow into your life. This energy has to do with allowing abundance, prosperity, health, and well-being into your life. In other words, you're not *forcing* anything; you are simply allowing, letting it flow, and receiving.

The energy of *Force* is an energy that creates effort, exhaustion, frustration, anger, fear, and separation, and it actually takes energy away from *you*. This energy has to do with how most people are living their lives, thinking they need to get busy and do so many things, creating frustration, anxiety, and stress in their lives. In other words, this is the energy most people use every day in their lives to try to *force* things to happen in their lives, vs. allowing them into existence.

It's very important for me to talk about this topic, as it helped me develop an awareness that allowed me to always be asking the following question:

"Where am I living my life from right now? Am I living from a place of Power, or am I living from a place of Force?"

I would love for you to ask yourself this question as many times as you can throughout the day. In the beginning, I remember asking myself this question every 5–10 minutes. And what I've found is that, without knowing it, I was living my life from a place of *fear (force)*. When you take your own life as an experiment, life becomes so much more fun!

Force – Living in Fear

Force resides outside of you. Think of *Force* as the energy you put *out* there whenever you try to make something happen. It is the energy you use when you try to change your outer world using an **action** (like trying multiple ways to get whatever it is that you want: calling someone that hasn't replied to your text, forcing someone to do things your way, working extra hours to get a promotion, etc.). *Force* is the energy you use every time you go out the door thinking you *need* to go to work, because otherwise, how else are you going to *survive* and pay the bills? *Force* is the energy you are using when you say things like: *"I have tons of things to do today."* You live today as if you were trying to *fix* what *broke* yesterday.

We have been brought up to live in the energy of *Force*. Whenever you are "forcing" something, it tends to *not feel natural*, and it isn't. You might not know this, but you are living through the energy of *Force* most of the time. You *"work hard"* to get that promotion: You stay long hours at work to prove to your boss that you are a good employee, you tell your partner that things should be a certain way (your way), etc.

Love vs. Fear

Force will always make you feel exhausted and tired at the end of the day. Force will take your energy away. Anything like arguing with someone, trying to control your kids' or spouse's behavior, trying to force an outcome, rushing from place to place to keep doing more things, etc., is using the energy of *Force*. *Force* is what wars are based on—who has the "strongest" army. *Force = doing*.

You do not need to do anything; **you are everything.** And when you change into the energy of *Power*, things start flowing to you. You understand that you do not need to *do*, but rather *be*.

Force will always leave you feeling tired, exhausted, and lonely. *Force takes* your energy away.

Power – Living in Love

Power resides within. The energy of *Power* is the Magic Spark we have been talking about throughout this book. It is the energy you use when you change your outer world from within.

Power is when you align yourself with who you truly are. It is allowing abundance into your life. *Power* is understanding that because you are part of a Divine Source, you are loved, you are taken care of, and you do not *need* anything. *Power* is when you allow things to come to you (you do not chase them). *Power* is when you stand still and *know* everything is going to work out. **You do NOT need to do anything** for things to work out in your favor. (I understand this might seem hard to believe, but we have been programmed to believe that *we need to do something in order to get something in return*—this is a limiting belief.)

When you feel good about yourself, when you feel full of *love* energy, things flow easily and effortlessly to you. I am sure you can remember a point in your life where you felt like nothing could go wrong; you felt blessed. You were achieving things so easily. Everything was working out for you—you got the job, the date, and you even found money on the street—everything, as if by magic. You were living your life in the energy of *Power.*

Power will always leave you feeling joy, happiness, peace, and joy. *Power* always gives you energy.

Choosing *Power* or *Force*

When you do anything from the energy of *Power*, you feel energized, you feel passionate, you feel love for life, and you feel abundant. *Force* makes you feel weak and tired. *Force* is doing; *Power* is being. *Force* is happening every time you try to accomplish something from a place of lack. It happens when you say: *"I have to...," "I need to...," "I should...."* *Power* is felt from within, knowing that you are worthy of receiving. When in *Force,* you feel victimized by life; when in *Power,* you feel the creator of your life.

The energy of *Power* gives you energy. The energy of *Force* takes energy away from you.

Love vs. Fear

Here are a few examples, based on these two energies, so you can better understand these two energies that exist in this physical Universe. Notice which energy you normally use. Create that awareness. Simply make a decision where you want to stand, and remember:

Power will always make you feel strong. Force will always make you feel weak.

Power (High Vibration) vs. Force (Low Vibration) Human Patterns

- Love – Fear
- Giving – Taking
- Relaxed – Tense
- Being – Doing
- Calmed – Stressed
- Peaceful – Aggressive
- "I am enough" – "I need"
- Grateful – Life is not fair
- Confident – Arrogant
- Creator – Victim
- Natural – Artificial
- Balanced – Extreme
- Equal – Superior
- Bliss – Lack
- In love with life – Hatred toward life
- Life is easy – Life is hard

- Tolerant – Prejudiced
- Gifted – Lucky
- Spontaneous – Impulsive

    … and many more

Chapter 6

Allowing Miracles into Your Life

Allowing Miracles Into Your Life

Please be open to what you are about to read in this chapter. The following pages are life transforming as you allow yourself to see that this world is not really what it appears to be. The following chapter may take a couple of reads to understand the depth of what has been written. This specific chapter is meant to open your heart, mind, and eyes to realize that there is so much to realize and study about the way *life* really is. This chapter holds the key to understanding that abundance is all there is, and that miracles and real magic are for those who **allow** themselves to receive what's already part of our birthright. I hope you allow yourself to do this as well—magic is real.

Levels of Consciousness

In his book, *Power vs. Force*, Dr. David R. Hawkins introduced his fascinating Map of Consciousness to the world. Using a technique called *muscle testing*, Dr. Hawkins conducted over 250,000 calibrations over a period of 20 years of research. This research helped define a range of attitudes, values, and emotions that correspond to levels of consciousness. This range of values—along with a logarithmic scale of 1 to 1,000—became the Map of Consciousness. The intention behind mapping the different points and levels of consciousness, is so you and I can understand what the levels are, which level we currently *are* at, and be able to use this information so we can heal, recover, and evolve to higher levels of consciousness and energy. This is a fascinating read.

The Map of Consciousness starts at the lowest point, with shame, guilt, and apathy (all low energy levels that relate to

The Magic Spark

depression), and it goes all the way up to love, joy, peace, and enlightenment (states of human consciousness that only a few, such as Gandhi, Buddha, and Mother Teresa, have managed to achieve in a lifetime). The most interesting and fascinating realization I had about all of this, is that each level of consciousness carries within itself patterned thoughts, feelings, and emotions (energy) that will only perpetuate more thoughts, feelings, and emotions that correlate to the particular level of consciousness in which you currently sit—in other words, **you can only experience more of the same level of consciousness in which you find yourself. Let me expand on this...**

For example, if you are currently in the level of consciousness of *anger*, you will only be able to **think, feel,** and **act** on that level; it is as if you are trapped here. This level of *anger* carries within itself more thoughts, feelings, and behaviors that perpetuate more *anger* in you, and no matter what you do, you can only see *anger*. It is as if you became contaminated with *anger,* and the only thing that you can see, think, or feel is more *anger. Anger* becomes your state of being—you are now stuck in that vibrational trap, and you start to *catch* other thoughts, feelings, and actions related to that level. These thoughts, feelings, and actions exist outside of you, but you catch them, just like a virus, and they now come inside of you because *anger* is all you can experience.

When in the level of consciousness of *anger,* you will only be able to *think the thoughts* to create more *anger*. You will only be able to *feel the feelings* to create more *anger*, and you will only be able to *act with the actions* to create more *anger*. It is as if you have *anger-lenses* on, and you are only capable of seeing, feeling, and acting more *anger*. It is as if you are blind to any other emotion.

This pattern of *anger* is so intense that you start to attract into your life other people, experiences, and circumstances that find themselves in that same level of consciousness in which you are currently living, only to match yourself with them and create even more *anger* in this case. It would be impossible for you to attract *love* when you are in the level of consciousness of *anger*. It would be impossible to experience *peace*, *joy*, or anything else while being in the level of consciousness of *anger*.

There are only two ways out of the level of consciousness in which you are currently living at the moment, and that is:

(1) You must become aware of which level you currently find yourself in, so you can move up the ladder one level of consciousness at a time. Your awareness and your attention are key for this.

(2) You simply **let go** of the level where you find yourself in. You develop the emotional and spiritual intelligence to understand that the Magic Spark within you can absolutely make you transcend any *bad* level of consciousness that you do not desire to experience. By connecting to your Magic Spark, and the more you are in touch with it, you are reminded that love, happiness, peace, abundance, and joy are your natural state of being, and everything that is happening *outside* of you is simply an *illusion* of the ego—an *illusion* of separation—that is not real. Because you are not a victim of what happens to you, you are the creator of what happens to you. More to come on how to do that quantum leap!

In my group coaching and online courses, we practice and study the exact formula on how to do this. There is a process you must go through to "let go," so you can become a new self and start living your life from the higher levels of consciousness. It is beautiful to see how there are students that are regaining the ability to direct their own life in the direction of love, happiness, peace, joy and abundance.

Here's another way to look at it. If you are feeling *angry*, for example, you will automatically (without even wanting to) start to think more thoughts that will fuel your *anger* (this is called "spiraling"). Other thoughts and feelings will be triggered inside of you in order to perpetuate that original feeling of *anger*. You might be feeling *angry* for a specific reason (reason A), but out of nowhere, an entirely different thought will jump into your awareness (reason B) to perpetuate and make you feel *angrier*, making you feel as if you are not in control of what you're thinking. And now you find yourself feeling even more *angry* than before, which then will **unconsciously** make you think of yet another reason (reason C), which has nothing to do with A or B, to make you even *angrier*. And unless you are able to become aware of what's happening, the cycle will continue...

I hope this is a major moment of realization for you. In the past, it was for me. It makes so much sense! Are you perhaps able to then see why the things that you have attracted into your life are of similar nature to the way you have been thinking, feeling, and acting? How could you experience anything different from what you are vibrating or *being* (the level of consciousness you are currently in)? How could I ask the Universe, Source, or God, to help me, if I am not in a position to feel anything less than the level of consciousness in which I am currently.

Don't worry; later, in Part III of this book, I will talk about what the process is to jump above any negative level of consciousness, and the process I went through to recover my connection to my Magic Spark. I will talk about surrendering, what that means, and how to jump back into your natural state of being—of love, joy, and peace. I will share with you my technique called "Stop fueling the fire," inspired by a letting-go exercise from Dr. David Hawkins. This technique is explained in Part III of this book.

What's really important for me right now is for you to understand that each level of consciousness is always at play with the **Law of Attraction**—attracting more thoughts, feelings, and actions, similar to the way you are currently feeling. Think about each level of consciousness as its own world, containing within itself infinite possibilities, experiences, and outcomes that are only similar in nature to the vibration or energy field of that particular level of consciousness.

Everything Is Happening at the Same Time

"The biggest lie we were ever told is that we are linear beings living linear lives. In fact, we are dimensional beings living dimensional lives."
– **Dr. Joe Dispenza**

The reason I explained the levels of consciousness is because of the following extremely important fact: **Everything is always happening at the same time!**

What does "everything is happening at the same time" mean?

Shame, guilt, apathy, grief, fear, desire, anger, pride, courage, neutrality, willingness, acceptance, reason, love, joy, peace, enlightenment—they are all happening at the same time. They are all present, right here and right now. In this very second, regardless of how you feel right now (e.g., angry), ***all of the different levels of consciousness are available to you.***

Right in this second, there is a person that is experiencing shame; another is experiencing guilt, and another fear, another courage, another love, another peace, and so on...I think you get the idea. Right here, right now, at *all times*, shame, guilt, apathy, grief, fear, desire, anger, pride, courage, neutrality, willingness, acceptance, reason, love, joy, peace, and enlightenment are all present and available for you to choose which level you want to live from—it is as simple as that—and each of them represents a different dimension, a different life. Depending on which level of consciousness you choose to live from, you will experience a completely different life.

You cannot live the same life living from the level of consciousness of fear, if you were to live from the level of consciousness of joy, and this is what is called "jumping into a different dimension."

Allowing Miracles Into Your Life

Let's say you are currently feeling *apathy*. The reason you are not able to all of a sudden feel a higher and more positive feeling, over a lower and more negative one, is **not because that new positive feeling isn't existent at the moment, and it isn't because that positive feeling is not available to you;** it's simply because *you choose to stay* in the current level of consciousness that you are currently living in. It is purely your choice, and this is very exciting!

This is not meant to make you feel any guilt, sadness, or shame; on the contrary, this is to empower you to see that you can easily move away from an energy of victimhood, into an energy of creation. *You* can choose to see this as what this really is: you having total control of your life (which you always had). And if you choose to stay in a lower level of consciousness, please be aware that you are the one choosing to stay there; you are no longer a victim of any circumstance—you are the creator of your own life experience.

As you practice moving up the levels of consciousness, please be aware that you might have created a strong habit (without even wanting to) to experience certain levels of consciousness. This is where **unconditional love** plays an important role in your life. Please be patient, be kind, and be loving to yourself. Everything in this journey of self-discovery is about being aware of your thoughts and feelings. It is about having the patience and love that a mother has when her child is learning how to walk—she is never angry, she is never impatient; she is simply in loving anticipation of the miraculous moment that's to come.

It might seem easier said than done, but the way to move into any level of consciousness is by using your true superpower: your

The Magic Spark

attention. Your attention is your true Magic Spark in action. Your attention is awareness in motion. Attention is consciousness itself. Attention is the God Force living inside of you. And now you know the truth.

Your Attention – Your Superpower

"The only thing that ever makes you feel bad is your attention to things unwanted."
– Abraham Hicks

Your *attention* is by far the greatest asset you have to change your life. After your *awareness*, your *attention* is where change can happen. Your *attention* is the game-changer you have been looking for—it is your superpower.

Let's take a look at what happens at a quantum level when you give your attention to something, or to anything:

When you place your *attention* on a specific thing (a good or bad thought, an image, a good or bad memory of the past, the news, Facebook, Instagram, etc.), you are gathering all of what you are made of—your *Life Force*, the spirit inside of you—and you are giving all that energy to that specific thing or event. What you are doing in that moment is ignoring everything else that exists in your life, and giving your *Life Force* away to whatever you are paying attention to.

So why is this important to understand?

If what you are giving your *Life Force* (your attention) away to is something in particular that is making you feel bad, stressed, angry, anxious, depressed, etc., then you are literally throwing your life away for those seconds—or minutes, hours, months, and sometimes years—that you keep your attention on something that you do not desire.

Are you able to realize that the time that you give away, through your attention, to the news, a bad past memory, an old victim story of yours, the bad weather, what the politicians are doing, that fight you had with that family member 6 months ago, etc., will never come back? And are you also able to see that whatever you give your attention to, you will create more of that in your life? In the past, if you have ever felt angry or sad or anxious, for example, it is because you were placing your attention on thoughts—or on specific circumstances—that were creating feelings of stress, anger, or sadness inside of you. You have the power, through your attention!

Now let's apply this to the fact that this is why you keep living the *same old life!* You are placing your attention on things that have now become a habit. Be honest with yourself and ask the following question:

What do "I" pay attention to the most during my day? Is it social media? Is it the *problems* in my life? Is it the *injustice* of the world? Is it knowing the latest trend on the pandemic?

This is my rule (and I hope you can use it, and that it works for you too):

The Magic Spark

To the best of my abilities (awareness), I don't allow myself to talk about, think about, feel, or watch anything that does not make me feel good, hopeful, inspired, and abundant. And whenever I catch myself noticing that my attention has drifted to something negative, I simply let go, forgive myself, and shift my attention to what I know will best serve my Dream Life—a book, a song, an inspiring quote, a visualization of my Dream Life—you name it!

Your attention will bring to you more of what you are paying attention to—this is a universal law. Your attention is your Magic Spark in action. Please be mindful of what you decide to give your attention to.

Your attention is another step in my 5-step formula on how to create magic in your life. And my clients are learning how to start living what I call a "Dream Life," right here and right now, by using their attention. This is why, in my course, "Creating Magic in Your Life," I go deep into how your attention might not be as sharply focused or as strong as you might want it to be. Your attention might become easily distracted by so many thoughts and topics that are lying around in your head. We must realize how important our attention is.

Right now, your attention might be as distracted and all over the place as a little puppy. The easiest way to know how focused your attention is, is to close your eyes and focus on your heart. How long can you focus on the **warm feeling of love**, before a different thought of any kind pops in, substituting your focus on your heart? Five seconds? Fifteen seconds? Three minutes? Ten minutes? Point proven?

Regardless of where your attention's current level is at, please know, as Dr. Joe Dispenza says: *"Where you place your attention is where you place your energy."* And for me, that energy he is talking about (your attention) is your entire existence, your *Life Force,* and you are giving it away to something—whatever you choose to.

I am simply suggesting to why not place your attention on the things that make you happy. Can you commit yourself to giving away your *Life Force*, your attention, only to the things that inspire you, make you feel good, and bring joy to your life? And to *everything else,* you can say, **"Thank you, but no thank you!"**

A Miracle Requires Faith

"Faith is taking the first step even when you don't see the whole staircase."
– Martin Luther King, Jr.

Let me get this out of the way right now: *Faith is a spiritual thing, not a religious thing.*

It is very important to create the distinction that *faith* is a spiritual thing. Faith is the ability to believe in what doesn't yet exist, being **completely certain** that it *will*. Faith is *the knowing* that what you desire already exists in the non-physical world—the spirit world—and the only reason it is not here in this physical world is because it is delayed by a glitch of how this Universe works. But

The Magic Spark

you can feel it, smell it, touch it, see it (in your imagination), and sense it.

The reason why most people have lost their faith in what they cannot see, is because 95% of the world's population has been hypnotized by the *materialist paradigm*. There are phrases that have hardened into *facts* in most people's minds *(which are not true; they are only ideas that have been repeated over and over)*, and they are what's destroying faith. These are phrases such as, *"This is all there is," "Things have always been this way," "This is how life is," "It is what you are supposed to do," "There is no other way,"* etc.

We got it all wrong from the beginning... It isn't *"seeing is believing"*. The formula to bringing miracles into your life experience, is reading this phrase backwards (pure faith): ***"Believing is seeing."***

I would love for you to know that in the past, I used to be very afraid about *walking in faith*—taking a leap of faith, the first single step into the direction of my dream—but since I have done it, I've realized that "the path appears on its own," as if by magic. This is true magic! I still feel fear, but something inside of me—my Magic Spark—knows that as soon as I take Step #1, I will be able to see Step #2, and it is not until I am standing on Step #2 that I will be able to see Step #3, and so on.

It has been such a miraculous experience to simply jump! And I want to encourage you to do it. You simply must take Step #1; that is all I ask. The reason you and I are afraid of taking a leap of faith, is because we want to see the ***10 Steps***—*the plan*—all perfectly lined up, before we can move into the direction of our dreams. But this is exactly why we freeze and never take action, because you will never be able to see Step #2 if you haven't taken Step #1.

I promise you that someone or something will catch you once you *take your leap of faith* (once you take your first step into the direction of your dreams). This is an experience that is almost impossible to describe; you can only experience it—it is meant to be lived. Just let your Magic Spark guide you one step at a time. Your miracle awaits in the *unknown*. And *faith* is your light in the dark.

> *"If you knew who walked beside you at all times, on the path that you have chosen, you could never experience fear or doubt again."*
> – Wayne W. Dyer

Spiritual Stewardship

This concept of *stewardship* was introduced to me by my good friend and mentor, James MacNeil, creator of Pure Spiritual Intelligence and the Dream Life Movement. It took me about 8 months to finally get it. He explained it perfectly, but now I know that it was me who wasn't ready to understand it. It is my hope that I am able to do justice to this concept, as it is essential for your *allowingness* in miracles.

Stewardship is *"the careful and responsible managing, conducting, or supervising of something valuable that is entrusted to one's care."*

So here is why this concept is so important in allowing miracles into your life:

- You desire more *free time*; am I right?
- You desire more *money*; am I right?
- You desire more *talents (to be more talented at a particular thing; to have more knowledge)*; am I right?

Here's the big question:

"Then what are you doing with whatever **(1) free time, (2) money, and (3) talents** that the Universe has entrusted you with so far?"

- What have you been doing with the *small amounts of free time* that you have?
- What have you been doing with the *small amounts of money* that you have?
- What have you been doing with the *small amounts of talents* that you have?

The Universe—through your Magic Spark—has already provided you with an amount (whatever that is, big or small) of **free time, money,** and **talents**. But are you being responsible with that?

Allowing Miracles Into Your Life

Whenever you have some *free time (even if it is 20 minutes a day)*: Are you getting caught in the black hole of Netflix or social media scrolling? Or are you making good use of that time to nurture your soul?

Whenever you have some **extra money** *(even if it's $50 a month)*: Are you soon spending it on the next *newly-advertised thing*? Or are you putting some of it into savings, some of it into education (the real kind), some if it into a never-touch pile, and some into treating yourself to something that would make you happy?

Your **talents** *(even if it's sharing a good story)*: Have you been hiding your Magic Spark, what your uniqueness is—in other words, what you are good at—for fear of *"what would they think"* or *"I am not good enough?"* Or are you sharing your talents, using your uniqueness to bless the world with who you really are, and giving your gifts away in service of others?

Please know that the Universe wants to give you more free time, money, and talents, but before it does, it wants to make sure that you can handle what you have already been entrusted with. And this is so clear once you are open to receive the lesson. It was a huge "aha" moment in my life! I can be completely honest and say that I was a terrible steward of my free time, money, and talents.

The concepts in this book are meant to create a new belief system that will help you become a "miracle magnet." These concepts are meant to move each and every single one of us from victimhood to creation! You and I have always had the power. The Magic Spark inside of us has always been there telling us all of this.

So, none of these concepts are meant to hurt; they are meant to liberate and awaken.

"This stewardship concept is meant to help you understand that you ARE the 'cause' in the Law of Cause and Effect. You can indeed cause an effect."
– **Rodrigo Diaz Mercado**

Chapter 7

The Gift That Keeps on Giving

"When you understand who you truly are, how extraordinary and magnificent you are, you understand that the nature of God is to speak through you."
– Rodrigo Diaz Mercado

Your Purpose – The Gift

"The two most important days in your life are the day you are born and the day you find out why."
– Mark Twain

Most people spend their entire lives trying to look for their life's purpose outside of them. You and I have been told to go find it *out there*. Or simply, you have been told to *find it*. This has created anxiety and stress in people's lives, as they feel the pressure to be something they are not, or to spend the majority of their time not knowing that by being YOU—*the real YOU*—you are living "on purpose."

Please understand this:

"By the sole fact that you showed up in this Universe, you have a purpose."

You are a ***gift*** to this world!

Every leaf, every wing, every cloud, every drop of rain—everything in this Universe plays such an important role in the balance of life. Everything from the largest scale, like the sun, to its smallest particle, like the gas we know as Oxygen—everything from big to small has a fundamental role and unique purpose in this Universe. Otherwise, it wouldn't be called Universe—"Uni" meaning "one."

There is a uniqueness to you that no one else could ever replicate. Even though you were raised to believe that you are *like everybody else,* I can never put myself behind your eyeballs to understand and see this life in the unique way that you do. Know this:

You are here to bring forward the unique way in which you see life. You are here in this world to uniquely express your Magic Spark into being. You are here in this world to be YOU—the real YOU.

Finding Your Purpose – Finding Your Gift

You are a gift that has a gift!

So, the question is: *"How to find your purpose?"*

Whether you already know and are on your way to living your life's purpose, or you are asking yourself the question above—wherever I caught you in your journey—I want you to know that *it is perfect.*

If you are looking for the answer to the above question, I am sorry to disappoint you, but you will not find it in this book, *or*

The Gift That Keeps on Giving

anywhere else for that matter. Your life's purpose is not something that needs finding; your life's purpose is something you simply allow from the inside out. And I am brave enough to say that *you already know what it is, even though you might think you DON'T.*

Here are two ways to nudge you to remember that you already know what your gift, your purpose, is:

Ask yourself these three questions, and answer them through your Magic Spark's voice:

1. "What did I really like to do when I was a kid (before you got brainwashed with the idea to study a career that will get you to a good paying job)?"

2. "If I had all the money in the world, and I knew I was financially covered for life—*"I did it"*—what projects would I be doing with my life?" (Please be honest here. Yes, the beaches and trips are fun, but at some point, you would stand up and try to give something back to others, through your purpose.)

3. "If I had 2 years left to live, what perspective would I want to pass on to this world and my loved ones? What would I do with my life with these last 2 years?" (Please be honest here too. Yes, you would travel; yes, you would quit your job, but what would you like to leave behind… what message?)

Living Inspired:

I've learned this from the beautiful teachings of Dr. Wayne Dyer. The word "inspired" truly means *"to be in spirit."* When you separate the word "inspired" in two, you can clearly see *"in-spirit."*

A good way to reconnect with your life's purpose, the way your Magic Spark wants to express itself, is to simply do the things that inspire you the most. Doing what inspires you—for example, playing music, dancing, cooking, painting, writing a book, etc.—is a *spiritual whisper* from your Magic Spark, letting you know that there is something here for you. Simply keep taking that feeling to the next level. Allow *spirit*—your Magic Spark's way of expressing itself—to keep on telling you where to go.

Last but not least, never put a time limit on *"finding your purpose."* As I mentioned before, you already know it. When you are happy, doing what you love and living inspired—*in-spirit*—you are already on purpose. Let your Magic Spark express itself how it wants; this is the gift you bring to this world, and we ALL WANT TO SEE IT—THE REAL YOU!

Living on Purpose – Giving Your Gift Away

You are a gift that has a gift, and a gift is meant to be gifted!

Your gift is not for you. You were given a gift so you can give it away. Divine Intelligence loves you so much that it gifted you

The Gift That Keeps on Giving

with your gift, your purpose. And it did this so that you can share it with others.

> *"We must realize that our life's purpose is best used in service to others. We came to this world to share our gifts with each other—that is the power of who we truly are— the Magic Spark acting within."*
> **– Rodrigo Diaz Mercado**

Funny enough, we are always looking for abundance, love, happiness, peace, joy, prosperity, more money, etc., and we miss the whole point of life: It is through serving others through our life's purpose that abundance, love, happiness, peace, joy, prosperity, more money, etc. flows easily and effortlessly, like a waterfall of miracles, into our lives.

What happens if we are just afraid to do so? As we saw in Chapter 2 (The Program), we have been trained to think: *"But what would they say if I don't follow the norm?"* or *"You cannot make money with your passion,"* or *"The only way to make money is to have a job"*... I would encourage you to challenge this "software" that was implanted in you, especially today. Millions of entrepreneurs have shown the world that there are so many ways to make money doing what you love, and that is only one of infinite possibilities.

The Magic Spark

It is also important to note that when you are doing what you love, when you are living your life through what your Magic Spark wants you to express, you are never tired. You don't seem like you are working. You are simply playing, creating, and expressing yourself. When you put your gift into action, you will never feel like you are exhausted, because it comes from your Divine Power. On the contrary, when you are doing something that is not aligned with your Magic Spark, your purpose, you will always feel tired, angry, and that life is unfair. (Does this sound familiar?)

And here is the last point on this:

What if the only thing this world needed in order to change to a world of pure love, happiness, peace, and joy, was to see what your gift is—the real YOU?

"You are a gift that has a gift, and a gift is meant to be gifted!
You are and have always been
THE GIFT THAT KEEPS ON GIVING."
— **Rodrigo Diaz Mercado**

You Are Verb, Not Noun

You are **verb** and not **noun**. This is an extremely important concept to understand on your way to finding your gift and reconnecting to your Magic Spark.

The Gift That Keeps on Giving

You are ***not*** a physical *thing*, you are ***not*** an "object," you are not a ***material*** thing. Even though you might identify yourself with a physical body, it doesn't mean that you are a physical object. What you are is ***pure "action"***; you are movement. You are ***energy in motion*** at all times. You simply *"are."* This is why you say "I Am..." The "I Am" that you are, never stops being. The "I Am" is an eternal thing. Let me explain this better...

The best way I can describe this so far, is the following:

You are a human **being.** This means you are always ***being*** something (I Am*)*. Every moment, you are ***being*** something (I Am something*)*. You never stop ***being*** something (you never stop *being* you at any point in your life).

Through your awareness, you decide what you ***"are"*** (I Am "X"). Every second of every day, you have the power to define yourself through your "I AMness" (I Am "X"). And **this is the secret to redefining yourself, to creating a new life.**

You can choose what you **"are"** at all times:

"*I Am* happy," "*I Am* sad," "*I Am* angry," "*I Am* at peace," "*I Am* abundant," "*I Am* poor," "*I Am* anxious," "*I Am* smart," "*I Am* dumb," "*I Am* healthy," "*I Am* sick," "*I Am* important," "*I Am* not important," etc.

"As human beings, we make the mistake of identifying ourselves with the 'human' in 'human being,' vs. understanding the truth: that we are the 'being' in 'human being.' You are energy! Energy never stops moving."
– **Rodrigo Diaz Mercado**

You are energy, and energy is always moving. It is always vibrating; it is never static. And if your cells are made up of energy, this means that the particles that constitute who you are, are always moving. Your cells are always in motion—this constitutes your *"I AMness."*

Chapter 8

Manifestation

Self-Actualization

"100% of nature goes for it..."
– James MacNeil

Have you noticed that 100% of nature goes for it? Have you noticed that an apple tree doesn't complain about being an apple tree, or that today it is raining, cold, or snowing? Have you noticed that an apple tree only knows how to be an apple tree?

How much does a tree grow per day? *As much as it possibly can...*

Why is it that as humans, we've forgotten that we are **nature** as well? Why is it that as humans, we've allowed our egos to take over and create excuses (illusions) to blind us from the truth: that we are here in this world with the only purpose to be everything we truly desire to be—to *self-actualize*.

You were placed in this world to be all you can possibly be. You were placed in this world to express the unique way you see this world. You were placed in this world to be a loving beam of light, manifesting all the desires that lie in the core of your heart. You were placed in this world to have a positive, loving impact on humanity, and to change the world of those around you. You are meant to do all of this by manifesting everything that lies within your heart, and this is why I wrote this chapter. Please, I invite you to be all you were meant to be. You are in this life to truly go for it! Now is the time, not tomorrow. Don't let your false self (your ego) get in the way. That little voice inside your heart (your Magic

Spark), telling you what you like, what you are good at, and asking you to go for it, was given to you as a guidance for you to self-actualize. Please listen to it, and... Go. For. It!

Choosing Your Reality

OK, let's talk about quantum physics, shall we? Ready for a big bite to swallow?

Everything you can ever imagine, desire, and wish for, exists as a possibility in the spirit world, the quantum field. And it does so because everything in the spirit world, and in this physical Universe, is energy. Everything in this physical Universe is energy that comes from the spirit world—the quantum field—and it is now arranged in a certain pattern. So for your wish, desire, and/or imagination to come true, energy simply needs to be organized in a specific pattern, for you to experience that particular desire, wish, and/or imagination as a reality in your life.

This is accomplished by using your awareness, your attention, your imagination, and your Magic Spark—this is the essence of "creating your reality."

Now let me explain that in a simpler way.

There are multiple experiences you can be having right now. You can say that there are multiple versions of you that are having a different life. For example, there is a *You* that is a multimillionaire, and there is a *You* that is not. There is a *You* that lives by the beach,

Manifestation

and there is a *You* that does not. There is a *You* that is healthy, and there is a *You* that is not. There is a *You* that has a brother, and there is a *You* that does not... (I think you get the idea).

There are multiple *You's*, living in different dimensions. They are all living a slightly different or a very different life from the one you are experiencing right now. What I am trying to say is that all experiences that exist as a possibility, are something you could actually experience in your lifetime. And somewhere, in a different dimension, there is a *You* that is living your particular Dream Life.

Please know this:

"All possibilities exist as a potentiality in the spirit world, and they can only be reached through the present moment and your wonderful human imagination."
– Rodrigo Diaz Mercado

Another way to look at this is by imagining different versions of yourself. For example, let's put a "number" to the different *Jenns* in this case; this might help illustrate my analogy:

Let's say **Jenn #1** is living the current life Jenn is actually experiencing. But there is **Jenn #45** living a more fulfilling life than **Jenn #1**. **Jenn #45** has a slightly better career, and she is healthier overall. But let's say there is also **Jenn #22,** who as a matter of fact is having a *more difficult* life experience. **Jenn #22** is battling a disease, she doesn't have a lot of financial support, and her

The Magic Spark

relationship with her family is not the best. **Jenn #22** is sad and angry most of the time. If you are still with me, there are infinite realities Jenn could be living.

Here is the juicy part. Now imagine there is **Jenn #37,** an extremely successful (however Jenn defines success), happy, healthy, loving, wealthy, abundant woman, who is currently living **Jenn #1's Dream Life.** **Jenn #37** has a beautiful relationship with her family, and she lives her entrepreneur dream, which allows her to do more of what she loves, and she is even giving back to the community out of pure love. **Jenn #37** has the perfect life.

Currently, **Jenn #1** is not living what **Jenn #37** is. And **Jenn #1** wants to live **Jenn #37's** life. Well, she can… and you can too (I obviously mean you can live your own Dream Life, not Jenn's #37 life).

But how do you choose the reality you want to live, and actually experience it? (Keep reading.)

Your Wonderful Imagination

"In order to live the life you've never lived, you must think the thoughts you've never thought before."
– Rodrigo Diaz Mercado

The concept you are about to read is a concept that I've been working with for quite a bit now. And I would love for you to be open to something new, to something you might have never heard before:

"Your imagination is Divine Intelligence itself (God Force, Creation Power) inside of you."

How could it not be? Human beings are the only ones who have the ability to imagine. Imagination is a Divine Gift. Imagination is not a children's thing or a creative person thing. Imagination is a God Force–a divine force–inside of you, with the **unlimited** ability to point you in the direction of unlimited possibilities. There are no limits to what you can imagine; there are no limits to imagination! Imagination is *omnipresent (you can imagine yourself to be anywhere in time and/or space)*; it is *almighty (everything can be imagined being done or created),* and it is *all knowing (you can imagine an answer to everything; if you can't, you allow it to come to you!).* No other living thing has this power. Imagination gives us the ability to travel in time to both the past (a memory) and the future (a possibility)!

Imagination is a Divine Gift; it is a spiritual thing. It is also your Magic Spark in action.

One of the Laws of Abundance is the Law of Creation:

"Everything in this physical world comes from the non-physical."

The Magic Spark

Your imagination is your tool to manifestation. Everything in this physical Universe was first imagined: your phone, your computer, cars, buildings, the internet, electricity! Everything was first imagined. Someone had to first see it inside their own invisible world before it became visible. As Dr. Wayne Dyer once said:

"You were not given the power of imagination, without also being given the power of creation."

Therefore, the first place where you need to see your desires come to life, is inside your wonderful human imagination.

"It is only once you imagine what your desires are, and how they feel, that you can embody them."
– Rodrigo Diaz Mercado

Imagination is one of the steps in my own formula on how to create magic in your life. If you would like to see the complete 5-step process, you can download my FREE eBook, *How to Create a New Personal Reality*, at **happylivinginstitute.com/ebook**.

It is only once you have imagined your wishes fulfilled that you are able to embody the state of being that you have created from within. This is the key to manifestation, understanding that your imagination is a tool that you are taking for granted by thinking it is just a child's state of being. Your imagination is *God, the Universe, Divine Intelligence,* in you.

"For life makes no mistakes and always gives man that which man first gives himself (through his/her imagination)."
– Neville Goddard

Your Awareness of Being

"You can only live the life of who you are aware of being—in other words, that which you identify yourself with."
– Rodrigo Diaz Mercado

This is a key concept to understand in order to be able to live the life you want to live—your Dream Life. You must be really honest here, and self-aware.

You are aware of being *you*—a teacher, a mom, a sister, a brother, a blue-collar employee, a social economic status, a person that likes "x," a person that doesn't like "y" (*or whatever you have identified yourself with*). This means that you can only experience the reality of who you are aware of being. If you are aware of being middle class, you will then only be able to experience the financial situation of being a middle-class *someone*.

Another example is, if you are aware of being someone that gets a cold every change of season, then you will always experience that which you have become *aware of being* and have identified yourself with—which is someone that gets a cold every change of season. Does this make sense?

So, my point is, if you want to manifest an experience or circumstance in your life, you must stop being aware of who you currently are—because you do not have that which you desire—and become aware of being of the person that is living your wish fulfilled. This means, for example, if you would like to earn fifty thousand more dollars a year, you must stop being the *awareness of being* that you are right now, and you must *embody* the *awareness of being* of a consciousness who is *right now* earning fifty thousand more dollars a year. You must become familiar, through your imagination, with how it feels to be the *awareness of being* of an extra fifty thousand dollars a year.

You cannot experience anything that you are not aware of being. You cannot lose the 20 extra pounds you would like to lose, because you currently are the *awareness of being* an extra 20 pounds. But when you start to embody what it feels like to be 20 pounds lighter, what it feels like to walk lighter, what it feels like to not have cravings, what it feels like to eat healthier, to feel healthy, etc., then you are **being the awareness** of that desire, **and that is when real magic happens! You must first become familiar with the awareness of your desire, before it can happen, because:**

"I AM, or the awareness of being, is the only reality."
– **Neville Goddard**

"I Am" is your *awareness of being*. If your awareness of being is:

"I Am poor," you will only experience the circumstances that will perpetuate the *awareness of being* of someone poor.

"I Am the way I am," you will only experience the circumstances that will perpetuate the habit of *being* who you *have been*.

"I Am a hard working person, barely making any money, and living in an economy that is hard," you will only experience the circumstances that will perpetuate that specific *awareness of being*.

You get the idea...

So, if you are currently not experiencing that which you truly desire, it is because you are not living in that new *awareness of being*. Change your *awareness of being* and you will change the world around you—it is a law of the Universe, and it works!

I never thought I would be able to write a book. My *awareness of being* was one of someone whose first language was not English, and of someone who was only able to think in pictures (as one of my masks was being a graphic artist). I used to say, "I am not good with words." Until one day, after an entire 5 years of feeling depressed, sad, angry, and anxious (an *awareness of being)*, I asked my Magic Spark—not knowing it existed back then—for guidance. I was willing to give up everything I had been up to that point; and it was only then that a new *awareness of being* came to be. I didn't know how, but I started practicing connecting with a new *awareness of being*.

The Magic Spark

Please keep this in mind: "How" things around you will change, is not up to you. If you focus on the "how," you will probably never get there. Allow the "how" to come naturally to you. Do not *force* the "how." As if by magic, things will appear in your life, once you have embodied that new awareness of being that which you desire.

I hope you understand that if you focus on the "how" of your desire, you are actually judging it. You are judging your desire and your new *awareness of being*. The second you have questions—"But how? How am I supposed to do that? How am I supposed to pay or have the money for that?"—you are limiting possibilities. The "how" is not up to you; the "how" is up to the Universe. You are only able to see very little compared to what the Universe—Divine Intelligence—can see. Your only *job* is to change your current *awareness of being* into the person who is already experiencing your wishes fulfilled.

Start identifying yourself—create a new self-image, a new *awareness of being*—with your desire, as if it is already happening.

My Manifestation Formula

Even though the intention of this book is to help you remember your way back to finding your Magic Spark, I can't help myself from sharing with you my personal formula to manifesting. This is what has worked for me so far. This is how I use my Magic Spark. And it is my hope that you start developing a manifestation practice that *you* like, because you are manifesting everything at all times, whether you like it or not, and whether you are aware of it or not.

Manifestation

I am always evolving these steps. I'm always researching and practicing new ideas and concepts to help me strengthen these "manifesting muscles."

Here is what I've discovered to be my manifestation formula. It helps me find peace every time I "lose" myself along the way. And it helps me manifest the miracles I have been blessed to experience.

It is my hope that this helps you become a more playful creator. Allow yourself to connect with infinite possibilities, as it is only when you are open to a miracle that a miracle happens. And please disconnect yourself from your analytical self—you have already analyzed, and over-analyzed, that which has not worked for you in the past. I am presenting to you an abundant mindset. I am presenting something to you that I call *Miracle Mindset*. I am telling you this from the bottom of my heart, as it was true for me, and it is true for you:

"We truly don't know what you and I are capable of. We have become experts at knowing what we *cannot do*, what we are *not good at*; we repeat this story over and over again. It is time to stop this pattern and be open to the idea that you and I are unlimited beings. We truly don't know what you and I are capable of; maybe it's time to find out..."

Step 1 – Imagination:

If everything already exists in the spirit world (which it does), it must simply first be imagined; otherwise, how else could you tap

The Magic Spark

into it? It must also be defined using your wonderful human imagination (God Force). It is through your imagination that just like an artist, you are able to shape and sculpt your masterpiece. Every defined thought you have about the specific person, outcome, and experience you want to manifest, is like one brushstroke on a beautiful painting, or a hammer and nail removing the excess of stone to discover the statue that lies within the big piece of rock.

You must imagine to the best of your abilities, and trust that each day you spend time imagining your Dream Life, you will find more and more details every time—find those details. If you don't define the details of your Dream Life (where you live, how big your house is, what color it is, the type of furniture it has, etc.), it's like going to a restaurant and telling the waiter: "Can you bring me food?" (The waiter will not know what to bring you).

Step 2 – Choosing a Reality:

Out of all the infinite possibilities that exist in the spirit world, out of the multiple versions of you, take the time to choose the one version of *you* that is living your Dream Life.

Remember that through your *attention,* you are also choosing at all times what version of *you,* you are living right now. Always ask yourself: "Would the person living my Dream Life feel frustrated in this situation? Would the person living my Dream Life watch the news channel that makes me feel fear and anger?"

Step 3 – Embodying That Reality (Let It Be Your New Self-Image):

This is a fun one. You must embody your chosen state of being. You must think, feel, and act as if what you desire was already here. You can have a lot of fun with this one. Through your imagination, you can embody today who you desire to be tomorrow. This is such an important step in the process of manifestation. Can you feel abundant and secure before your wealth shows up? Can you feel well and healthy before your healing shows up? Can you feel loved before your relationship shows up? This is the game of embodying your *True Self*.

The biggest challenge comes when something doesn't go the way you would have wanted it to go. But you must then stop, think for a second, and ask yourself: "How would my Dream Life self react to what is happening right now?" And to be completely honest, if you could have and be everything you have ever desired to be, do, or have, when you had been experiencing something that was not that pleasant, perhaps that version of yourself would be so full of happiness, love, and compassion that instead of getting angry at someone or at something, you would simply not let it bother you. It only bothers you right now because you have not yet embodied that new state of being.

Embody that perfect True Self, and your life will change; there is no other option—it's called the Law of Assumption.

Step 4 – Trust/Believe/Be Grateful (The Miracle Is Not up to You!)

"A miracle requires faith."

Faith is the ability to believe in what you cannot see, yet you know it is *there*.

You and I were not taught to trust and believe in ourselves, nor in this invisible world that is the origin of everything. It is such an irony, but the spirit world works the opposite of how you and I were taught to think (because we were taught to think through a program: materialism).

The formula is not *"see it to believe it,"* but rather, **"believe it to see it."**

You must act and live your life as if your desire has already happened. You must act, think, and feel as if you were living the reality you have already imagined, chosen, and embodied, regardless of what is going on in your current perception of reality. And you can only do this if you trust and believe that you already are that which you desire to be. And it is only then that miracles will start to happen unexpectedly.

"Change your conception of yourself and you will automatically change the world in which you live. Do not try to change people (or circumstances); they are only messengers telling you who you are. Revalue yourself and they will confirm the change."
– Neville Goddard

The above is also based on principles of neuroscience. When you truly believe and start acting as if what you desire has already happened, your body will create chemicals and toxins, inside of your body, to reflect the feelings that those experiences would give you. So, what you are doing is that you are hacking your brain and body to believe that what you desire has happened; therefore, because you truly believe at your core that the experience already happened, your unconscious mind will literally push your life experience into creating the circumstances, people, and experiences that will lead you to the fulfillment of your desire—as if by magic.

Step 5 – Ignoring the 3D (the World Outside of You):

This is one of the most important pieces of the puzzle. Whatever happens in your life that is not aligned with your desire, the best version of yourself, or your Dream Life (something you didn't like or a negative situation that happened), you must not pay attention to it—you must simply let it slide. You must simply stop fighting "what is," because "what is" **was manifested in the past.**

If you spend your Life Force reacting to "what is" (something you don't like or a negative situation), you are fighting a shadow. You are making your past more real than the possibility of your future. If you experience something you don't like, or a negative situation, and you give your attention to it, you are simply making it bigger and are putting all your God Force on expanding that which you do not want more of (what an irony).

And what you might not be understanding here is that ***the Universe is always on your side.*** So if something "negative" happened, it is only negative from your perspective. What I am trying to say is that if you would understand that the Universe—Divine Intelligence—always has your back, maybe *what happened* needed to happen for you to be pointed in the direction of your wish being fulfilled. But if you spend too much time fighting *the shadow of what happened,* you are missing out on the miracle in front of you—the direction where you need to go.

Chapter 9

Living in Abundance

Living in Abundance

Abundance Is All There Is

If I ask you to think about the concept of "duality," I think it is not a hard concept to get. Duality is the quality of having a contrast, an opposite. Our 3D reality is based on the concept of duality. For example, there is day and night, tall and short, happy and sad, cold and warm, etc. From a spiritual standpoint, duality is needed to experience happiness in your life; otherwise, how would you know what happiness is if you didn't have the contrast of sadness to compare it with; or how would you know what rich is if you didn't have the contrast of poor to compare it with... I think you get the idea.

It is said that duality is what makes this physical Universe exist, and I agree.

The exciting part is that I think I have found the only thing in this Universe that has no opposite and does not experience duality: **abundance**! Abundance is all there is! Abundance doesn't have an opposite. This means that abundance is one of the only truths of this Universe, as it transcends the limitations of this time-space continuum. I will explain why abundance has no opposite, before we go any further.

You might think that "lack" is the opposite of abundance, and I want to let you know that from my point of view, I don't think this is true. Are you ready for a big "aha" moment?

There is either an abundance of abundance, or an abundance of lack!

The Magic Spark

Abundance of Abundance –

This is where you **get more** of what you like. With this type of abundance, you get more of *"more."* This means that when you pay attention to happiness, love, peace, health, prosperity, etc., you will get more of the same.

Abundance of Lack –

This is where you **get more** of what you DO NOT like. With this type of abundance, you get more of *"less."* This means that when you pay attention to anger, stress, anxiety, lack, sadness, etc., you will get more of the same.

Can you see how, no matter which one you choose, you will always get more of the one you are paying attention to?! This is HUGE. This means that this Universe loves you so much that it is always being **abundant** toward you! It is always on your side! It is always giving you an abundance of abundance (more of *the more)*, or an abundance of lack (more of *the less)!*

Understanding this alone can actually change a life. I hope you are starting to see how powerful this concept is, as whatever you may pay attention to—abundance of abundance (more of *the more)*, or abundance of lack (more of *the less)*—the Law of Abundance says that you will get more of it... it's the law.

Abundance Is Your Nature

What Is Abundance?

Most people tend to think that abundance has to do with money; and even though it includes money, it is so much bigger than that. Abundance is a loving energy that has four characteristics:

- It never ends.
- It always gives.
- It doesn't judge.
- It only knows how to love.

The best example of abundance in this physical Universe is the sun itself. The sun doesn't judge (it doesn't say "you over here get light/heat, but you over there don't"). It always gives heat and light (it doesn't stop giving). It never ends (no one knows when it started, and it never stops). And it only knows how to love.

I want you to understand that you are an abundant being by nature. You, like the sun itself, have these four characteristics (you have the ability not to judge, you never end, you can always give, and you know how to love). This is what being abundant means: to be in a position where you *know* you already are blessed, and that you are here on this planet to share yourself and your love with others. You don't *need* anything. The only thing you "need" to do is to breathe and drink water...

Abundance Is a Four-Legged Table –

An abundantly balanced life is like a four-legged table. In order to live a true abundant life, you must understand how abundance works when we talk about "human life." Abundance has these 4 pillars, and you must become familiar and grow in each one, in order to have an abundant life:

Love – This is your relationship with yourself and your divinity. This kind of love is between you and you alone (your divinity—the Universe, God if you will).

Relationships – This one has to do with your relationships with everyone else outside of you: your partner, your family, your friends, the world around you.

Health – This is the understanding that if there is no health, it is very hard to enjoy life. If you are not healthy inside, and you live in survival mode all the time, life becomes a struggle. Health is essential to living an abundant life.

Prosperity – This is where financial abundance, money, and your purpose fit. Money should always be present in your life as it is natural to have a flow of money that will circulate to you and from you, in order to cover your needs and more. The amount of money that is present in your life has nothing to do with the economy, or your boss, or your level of education; it has everything to do with your level of consciousness and awareness about wealth and prosperity. Do you believe it is hard to make big amounts of money? Do you believe it is hard to get a good paying job? Do you believe you "need" to work to make money? **Whatever it is that you believe, your subconscious mind (the Universe in you) will find the evidence to make your beliefs a reality.**

Your purpose also fits in this category, as when you put your purpose (your gift) in serving others, you are destined to live an abundant life (both in a financial and prosperous way).

It is essential that you start living your life from a different perspective, knowing that you are already an abundant being, and that you came into this world to express and flow that abundance through you. You are not a victim of any circumstance. Stop being a "this is good or bad" kind of person—I invite you to be a *results-oriented* person. If you currently are experiencing something you don't like, look at it as a result. YOU can always change the result, through your awareness and consciousness, through going inside.

"The Universe/God cannot give you anything, nor do anything for you, as IT can only do things through you."
– **Rodrigo Diaz Mercado**

Living an Abundant Life

Living an abundant life is a simple decision that most people don't want to commit to nor take. I am going to share with you **4 very simple steps** to living an abundant life. If you are able to commit to and follow these 4 simple steps, you are destined to live an abundant life. *Are you up to the challenge?*

The Magic Spark

Four Steps to Live an Abundant Life:

Don't Complain – An abundant being doesn't complain! An abundant being doesn't see lack; therefore, he/she can't complain, because *lack* is not part of his/her awareness.

Don't Envy – Envy is the one emotion that keeps 80% of the population from abundance. Being envious means that you are looking at something on the outside, and making a judgement based on the fact that someone else is showing the evidence of having something you would like to have.

I must confess, in the past, I used to envy a lot, until I realized that envy was the one thing keeping me from being abundant. For example, someone in your company or on social media gets a promotion, the title YOU wanted... Don't feel envy; rather, celebrate the fact that the Universe is saying: "Look at this post in social media about this person's promotion. I am putting this post in your awareness so you can continue to dream about yours—yours is next!" It is all a matter of perspective. What do you choose to see? In the past, I used to see that "I didn't get that promotion." Today, I choose to see, "Wow, it is so close to me, and this post is evidence of it!"

Don't Judge – Here's the secret to not judging: Please understand that **a judgement is simply a wall you are putting up to cover a wound from the past.** A judgement is the comment you make when you are trying to cover up something from the past (conscious or unconscious) that hurt you. An abundant being doesn't judge, because he/she lives in the present moment, where love and abundance are the only things that can be present.

Living without Fear – An abundant being understands that fear is an illusion of the ego. Fear only exists because you are basing a decision on an imaginary future that is based on your past, and which is not even present. An abundant being understands that even if fear is present, it must be ignored, as it is not real—it is an illusion of the mind.

If you were to **not complain, not judge, not envy, and live without fear,** you would truly live an abundant and prosperous life. I guarantee that! These are four very simple decisions that almost no one is willing to live by. *Are you up to the challenge?*

Gratitude 3.0

Gratitude is a topic that tends to be overrated because it is not understood. If you truly understood the power of gratitude, you would spend every second of your life in the awareness of feeling gratitude. This is why, today, I am writing about it!

Gratitude alone can change your life. And I hope that within the following paragraphs, I can help you see a new meaning to what this word means.

The thing about gratitude is that it has the "illusion" to be rooted in the Law of Cause and Effect. The Law of Cause and Effect says

The Magic Spark

that for every effect, there needs to be a cause. This means that in order for you to be grateful, you think that there needs to be something or someone that is the cause for you to be grateful. The understanding of this law has blinded people to not be happy right here and right now, as they are waiting for something on the outside (a cause) to change how they feel on the inside, and to fill them up with gratitude (the effect).

I am asking you to take the idea that gratitude is rooted in the Law of Cause and Effect and flip this law on its head. I am asking you to do it backwards and change it to the Law of Effect and Cause. Stay with me on this one...

I am asking you, right here and right now, to feel the effect *first* (gratitude); and let the cause appear on its own (the person or thing). I am asking you to be grateful for something that hasn't happened in the physical world but already exists in the spiritual world. Can you teach your body to be grateful for something that hasn't happened yet? If you can, then as if by magic, the thing you are grateful for will appear—it has to; it's the law!

Gratitude is to be grateful for what you have; so when the Universe senses that you are grateful for something, and the Universe sees that this something is not "physically present" in your life, the Universe will correct this discrepancy and create the physical experience in your life! This is real magic! Now, I can't tell you how fast or slow things will appear in your life, but I can assure you that they will, if you stay in gratitude.

Living in Abundance

You and I have been conditioned to behave through the Law of Cause and Effect: "I must get something first so I can then be happy." I am asking you to take this mathematical equation and flip it around (yes, in math you can flip things, and it works: 1+1=2 ... 2=1+1).

The whole gratitude principle alone can transform your life TODAY. The Universe will work with you to change everything around you, to give you the experience of what you are already grateful for.

Here is a new practice to start doing every night of your life; this will change your life.

The Three Levels of Gratitude –

Every single night, please practice these three:

Gratitude 1.0: "I am grateful for what happened to me..." (Especially the "negative," you can be grateful for the lessons from what happened.)

Gratitude 2.0: "I am grateful for what I have not experienced, but I know I will... (This is where you can start using your imagination and visualization to pull what you want from the spiritual world into this physical one.)

Gratitude 3.0: "I am grateful for what I have not experienced and that I don't even know I will... (This is where you are open to experience the unknown. This is where you are walking in faith, trusting that the Universe has your back, and that life is a perfect symphony that you are a part of, and that everything you are experiencing is perfect.) I am grateful that you are reading these words, and I hope to see you soon.

"Gratitude should be as normal as breathing."
– Rodrigo Diaz Mercado

Part III
The Way

Chapter 10

Reclaiming Your Magic Spark

The Pyramids of Life

What you are about to read is one of the most exciting personal discoveries I've ever had. It has been the sum of my life's work up until now. I think it is a beautiful way to understand why we have suffered in the past. For me, it is the "how" in "how to live a peaceful and happy life." I've always asked myself "how" I can find peace. Is there a formula? Could I teach it if there is one?

The following pages will reveal one of those things that once you see it, you can't unsee it. And the most fascinating part is that it was right in front of you this entire time, staring at you. The answers to finding peace have always been within your reach.

It is my hope that these next two diagrams give you a sense of awareness, understanding, and a clear map to continue your loving journey of self-love and personal growth. Please know that you are indeed finding the answers you are looking for; and reading this book is one of the many manifestations of that desire.

The Pyramid of Destruction

"98% of the people in this planet are spending 98% of their time on 98% of the things that don't matter."
– **Neale Donald Walsch**

Ninety-eight percent of people live their lives through "a someone"—an avatar they've created throughout the years, with labels such as mom (or dad), sister (or brother), woman (or man), a

The Magic Spark

certain ethnicity group, a certain age, a certain profession or job title, etc.

I'm confident to say that this is happening to you as well. As soon as you wake up, you go into what I am calling, right now, "your avatar"—an idea of a self, created by the labels you have chosen to identify yourself with (or perhaps you might think that you didn't choose them, but you did). Every morning as you wake up, you pick up "your life," exactly where you left it the day before: perhaps attending the kids, checking work emails and social media... You jump out of bed, and you rush to your *daily hustle* without thinking about it.

What you might try to do after you have gone through that *daily hustle*—your giant to-do list for the day (chores, kids, work, etc.)—is to try to spend some time, at least 30 minutes, on yourself (that's if there's any time left in the day whatsoever). But when you finally get to those glorious, personal 30 minutes, you are extremely tired; you are exhausted, and there's nothing left in the tank for your self-love time.

So you end up either watching Netflix for a couple of hours, or scrolling through your phone and going into the black hole of social media. You then go to bed, promising yourself that tomorrow will be different, only to find out that it is the same as yesterday. Believe me, I totally understand this; I have been working at creating a new life myself. And getting out of this habitual cycle is extremely important.

This next diagram is what I call **The Pyramid of Destruction** (Figure 1.1). And this is a simple yet profound representation of how 98% of people live their lives.

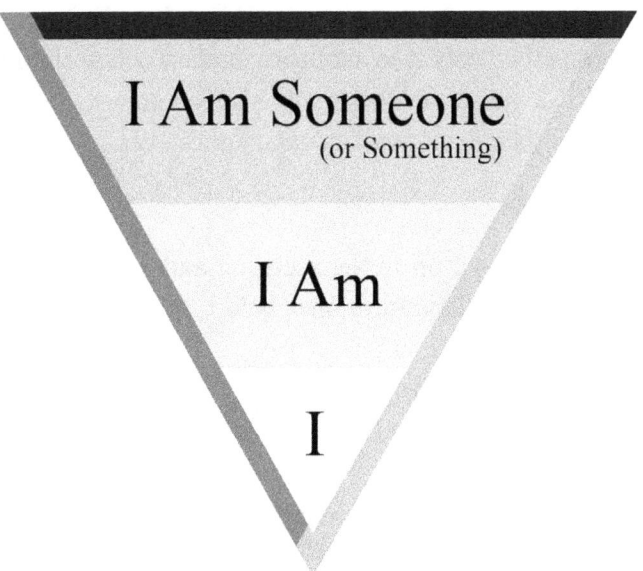

The Pyramid of Destruction *Figure 1.1*

The Pyramid of Destruction (Figure 1.1) is an inverted pyramid that has three levels. At the top is the "I Am *someone or something."* At the middle level, there is "I Am." And at the bottom, there is simply the "I."

The Pyramid of Destruction is meant to be read from top to bottom, with the first level being the top level: I Am *someone or something,* and the third and last level being the one at the bottom: "I."

I Am "*Someone or Something*" –

The "someone or something" is describing a *role* you tend to identify with in society. Most people, as soon as they open their eyes in the morning, jump into a *role* that they identify with. Some of the examples you previously read about are mother, father, sibling, job title, ethnicity, a gender identification, an economic status, a boss, an employee, or a lack of one, and sometimes even an illness or a body pain, etc.

Most people wake up in the morning and jump right into a role/identity/label. And as I mentioned before, there is a 98% chance that this is happening to you.

I Am –

This is the "being" in human being. This is the beingness we talked about in Chapter 7 (The Gift That Keeps on Giving.) You are a verb and not a noun; you are not the "someone or something" mentioned in the previous step of the pyramid—you simply *are*.

"I Am" are the most powerful words you could say in any language. And what follows after "I Am" is a command that you are giving to your subconscious mind. "I Am" is in present tense, and the present moment is all there is. It is the only place in time where you can create a new life. One present moment comes, and as soon as it comes, it is also gone; and so the next one comes into birth, followed by its own death, and so on.

"I Am" is *all there is* in this physical world, and it is your connection to the spiritual world.

"I Am" is all you can ever be—every second of every moment, you simply *are*. And you, through your awareness of *being*, define what you *are*—this is called your "I Amness."

The "I Am" in the pyramid is fulfilled by **feelings**. And this is why *feelings are the secret* of (1) manifesting your desires, and (2) allowing yourself back into being a peaceful, loving, happy, and abundant self.

In order to practice this "I Am" that I'm talking about, you must close your eyes. Connect with your heart and simply start feeling your True Self. I describe in depth this "I Am" practice, later in the exercise portion of this book. But essentially, you are to close your eyes and start *feeling*:

"I Am love," "I Am abundance," "I Am healthy," "I Am worthy," "I Am unlimited," "I Am prosperous," "I Am happiness itself," "I Am peaceful," "I Am…," etc. Every second that you feel "I Am (insert feeling here)", you define a new reality, whether it is a good one (a good feeling) or a bad one (a bad feeling), and whether you are aware of it or not—this is up to you.

I –

This is the level that only 2% of the population has allowed themselves to genuinely feel. The "I" at the bottom of the pyramid represents *oneness*; it is *wholeness*. The "I" at the bottom of the

The Magic Spark

pyramid is Divine Intelligence within you. This is the place where you stop *being* someone or something (you become no one and no thing, in nowhere), and you pay attention to the fact that what you truly are is a community of 50 trillion cells, "glued" together by the consciousness you call "you"—only that this consciousness is nothing else but pure Divine Intelligence. This is the *real you*, the invisible self that doesn't have a name or a shape; you simply can't grab it, yet you can feel it.

This consciousness can be felt by closing your eyes and paying attention to the *awareness of being*—feeling that you are aware of being aware. One of the biggest realizations you can have is the fact that this consciousness, this Divine Intelligence that lives in every single one of your 50 trillion cells, is the same consciousness that lives in the cells of every single person, animal, plant, and empty space in this entire Universe. **And once you pay attention to this consciousness, this Divine Intelligence that lives in everyone and everything, by expanding your awareness to** *feel it all,* **you are NOW feeling the "I" at the top of the pyramid.**

The "I" at the bottom of this pyramid is what true meditation is all about. Meditation is all about *feeling* Divine Intelligence; it is about *hanging out* with Infinite Intelligence and simply *being*. There's no agenda. You are not asking for anything; you are simply feeling the Divine in you. You are feeling loved, at peace, relaxed, and grateful. You go beyond your name, gender, age, nationality, job title, etc. **You go beyond form into the black space behind your eyes, and you simply feel Divine Intelligence inside and all around you.**

The Pyramid of Creation

This next diagram is what I call **The Pyramid of Creation** (Figure 1.2). **This is the answer to finding peace in your life.** This is what only 2% of the population in this world does, and what they commit themselves to do in order to live from their highest selves.

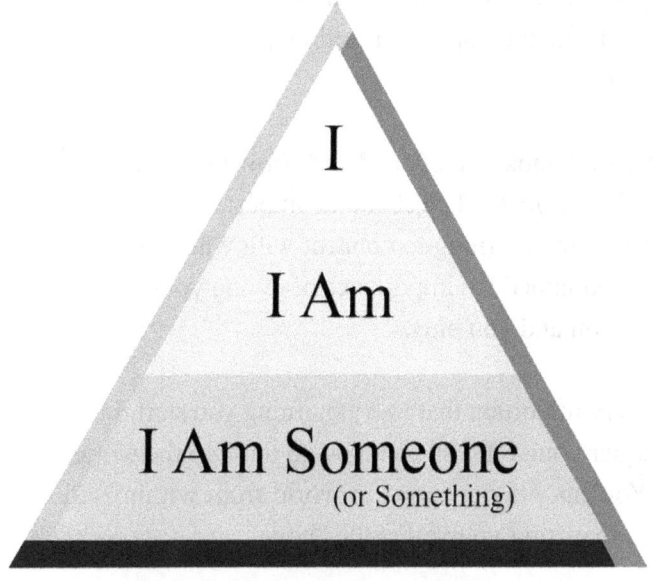

The Pyramid of Creation *Figure 1.2*

The Pyramid of Creation is the way to finding peace in your life. This is the way to manifest your desires.

As you can see, *The Pyramid of Creation* really is *The Pyramid of Destruction,* upside down. This means that you must start your day at the top level of this pyramid—with the "I"—and then move to the second level, the "I Am," and lastly moving to the bottom level of "I Am Someone or Something." This is how to reconnect with your true power, your True Self.

I encourage you to start living your life from the top of this pyramid, moving into the next level, and so on. In the following pages, you will find several practices that will help you start living your day from the top of this pyramid (The Pyramid of Creation), and NOT from the top of the other pyramid: The Pyramid of Destruction.

In my first book, *Sleight of Mind: How to Create & Experience Magic in Your Life*, I talked about the importance of creating a space very early in the morning to connect with who you truly are, your divinity. I explained the importance of giving yourself this time and space, for you and you only.

It is very important that every morning you start this way. When you conquer yourself, you can now go out into the world and serve others. You can only create your world from within; and this time that you are gifting yourself is the "how."

Changing *What Is*

There are two very important concepts to get from where you are to where you want to be:

You must stop fighting "what is."

You must find a personal time to reconnect with your True Self—with your Magic Spark.

Stop Fighting "What Is"

In order to start reconnecting with your True Self, you must first stop fighting "what is." Whatever it is that you are experiencing at the moment, is what's happening; it is what it is.

In other words, you must accept "what is". With this statement of "accepting what is," **I am NOT saying that you should conform or accept the negative circumstance that you are going through as your *reality, identity,* or *destiny*.** What I am saying is that you must take a deep breath and **stop fighting "what is."** The more you fight "what is" (by giving it your attention, your God Force), and the more you resist what's happening, the bigger and stronger it gets, as you are paying attention to it.

My intention with saying that you must accept "what is," is for you to (1) simply stop paying attention to the pain, or the cause of it (even though I understand that this might be difficult; while you might have pain in your body, you must become a person who can transcend that level of thinking), (2) don't judge yourself by saying anything like "why is this happening to me?" or "I shouldn't be having this pain anymore...," etc., and (3) *know* that this Loving Intelligence is always with you at all times. It has never left you, even though you might feel like you are alone in your darkest moments. (You are not—Divine Intelligence is still within.)

Do your best at simply taking a long, deep breath (3 or more if needed, for as many times throughout the day as you may need), and stop judging and condemning any negative or painful situation you might be going through. Do not have any opinion about it; stop saying, "This shouldn't be happening," or "Why me?" or "This is not fair," or "I hate that this is happening to me," or "I wish this wasn't happening to me," etc. All of those are labels and judgements; simply do not have any opinion on the matter. That is step one.

Personal Time, Personal Space

The second step to transforming yourself is creating personal time, where on a daily basis, you can go within and plant the seeds for a new you. A change never happens on the outside. You must first create it inside; you must identify yourself with a new *mind,* a new *you.* You must go from one level of consciousness to another (the one desired). And you can only accomplish this form the inside out.

"A flower blossoms from within; and so do you."
– Rodrigo Diaz Mercado

Protect a time and a space for you to reinvent yourself. You create yourself in the invisible world (spirit world), and you then experience its reflection in the visible world (physical Universe).

It is very important to have a space where you can learn to explore this invisible part of yourself. Through your imagination and a meditation practice, you are allowing yourself to discover parts of you that you haven't been familiar with. How else are you supposed to create a new life? You must first define what that new life, that new person, looks like in your imagination. You must define how that version of you thinks, feels, and reacts. What does this individual do for a living; who is this individual surrounded by? What types of experiences does this person have?

You must also protect a time where you can connect with your Magic Spark, this Divine Intelligence—a space and time where, as you go within, you connect to that eternal universal Source Energy. If you could simply close your eyes and feel "space," this Loving Presence is always there, waiting for you to recognize its warming nature that surrounds you from the outside and gives you life from the inside.

You came from a Divine Source of love, and when you stop identifying yourself with your labels, and you begin to identify yourself with your Source, you are allowing the flow of well-being into your life. You are allowing your birthright of abundance, love, happiness, peace, health, and joy into your life. What you identify yourself with is what you will manifest. You are Source, having a physical experience. Don't fall into the illusion of thinking you are a physical body that has a name, a job title, a nationality, all these "problems," and/or had a rough upbringing (even though you might have experienced one). Because whatever you identify yourself with, you will manifest more of the same. First and foremost, you are a spiritual being; you are part of the Divine Intelligence that created this Universe—you are part of this Divine Source. You are this Universe looking at itself.

"There are two births that must take place within a lifetime. The first one is the birth of God (Source Energy) as man. The second one is the birth of man as God (Source Energy)."
– Rodrigo Diaz Mercado

The exercises you are about to read were written with the intention to help you reconnect with your natural state of being, which is one of love, happiness, peace, and joy. These are the techniques that helped me climb the levels of consciousness. They help me find peace. I think about them and practice them over and over again, for as long as I can, whenever I can.

There is no wrong way to do this. You can choose to do one of them at any point of your day, or you can choose to do more than one in one day. It is crucial that you take time, **every day**, to remember who you truly are. Remember that **you are not** your name, gender, age, nationality, profession, or any other label you have picked up and believed along the way from the outside world. Who you are (rather "what you are") is the invisible part of you that looks at the outside from the inside. You are pure God Force; you are life. You are a miracle.

Being love, happiness, peace, and joy is a practice that will get stronger as you do it. Just like the gym, where you go to build strong muscles to be healthy and active, you must go to your mental-spiritual gym inside your heart and mind, where you take the time to build the muscles of living life from your natural state of being of abundance.

Please be patient with yourself. Whatever you are able to feel and imagine is perfect. The more you explore these exercises, the more you will find out about yourself. If you want to modify any of them to best fit your own practice, by all means please do so. These are all meant to help you "unlearn" the limiting beliefs and/or thoughts that you might have picked up along the way.

It is with all my love that I write these here for you.

I do ask one thing from you though: As you are doing any one of these exercises, please let go of your past. Please let go of who you have become to believe you are. **Do not bring into your imagination any thought that makes you feel bad**. And if a negative thought pops in your head, acknowledge it, look at it for a second, and let it go (go back to paying attention to the exercises below). Bring your attention, your superpower, back into the present moment, because it is only in the present moment that you are not any of your past labels; it is only in the present moment that you can begin to heal your life.

"The present moment is all you ever have."
— **Eckhart Tolle**

The Magic Spark

It is my genuine desire that, every day, you remember to identify yourself with the God Force that lives inside of you. You are beautiful. You are perfect. And if you could simply feel how magnificent you are... If you could fully remember who you truly are, or rather what you are, and what it took for you to be right here, right now, all your doubts would disappear, and all fear would be gone. You are the entire Universe, collapsed in one point in space and time. You are creation itself. You are magnificent. You. Are. Everything.

Chapter 11

7 Spiritual Practices to Reclaim Your Magic Spark

#1 Abundance

This is a beautiful exercise that has helped me understand what abundance truly is. Not only that, but it has also helped me get in touch with my Magic Spark—my own abundant self, and the abundance that radiates within me.

As you read through the next meditation, please be open to identify yourself with the words on the page. Connect with the feelings of what you are reading. As you find your sweet spot, you will start to feel more at peace. The goal is to stop identifying yourself with who you are not (feelings of stress, fear, anxiety, anger, and sadness), and start identifying yourself with your True Self. The most important thing is that when you do this exercise, you will be connecting with the stream of well-being that is always present. You are aligning yourself with this God Force that is loving, beautiful, abundant, creative, expanding, and kind. You are being who you truly are.

Having some classical or meditative music (preferably no one is singing, as it could be distracting) is very helpful. Set aside at least 5 minutes to imagine and connect to the following. (The longer you are able to spend with this thought, the more powerful this could be for you.)

The Sun –

Imagine the sun floating in the Universe. **Feel** how beautiful the light coming from it is. **Feel** how loving the heat coming from it is. Make a conscious understanding of how the sun does not judge.

The Magic Spark

It never says, "You over there get some heat and light, but you over there don't." It doesn't know how not to give light and heat. The sun is simply a never-ending source of warmth, light, and love (life). The sun simply "gives," and it never stops "giving," and **it never asks for anything in return.**

The sun never stops giving heat, light, and love (life). Just because you go to bed at night, doesn't mean that the sun stops being the sun. Just because you cannot see the sun, does not mean that it has "turned off." The sun keeps on *giving*. **This is the meaning of abundance. The energy of abundance comes from within, never from the outside. Abundance comes from within, and it never stops flowing. And just like with the sun, this is your true nature. Abundance like this, is your birthright.** The same abundant energy that created the sun, created you. It lives inside the sun and inside of you.

Once you are able to have a clear mental picture of what I've described, and can also feel the feelings of warmth, peace, and a loving energy, take some time to do the following:

From the outside in –

Feel how beautiful it is to receive this gift of love from the sun. Simply **imagine** that there is a wave of "love" constantly radiating toward you. Sense it with your awareness, with your eyes closed. Sense this with your skin. **Feel** this wave of "love" coming from the outside and gently touching your body. **Feel** the love, **feel** the joy; **feel** love touching you. **Feel** the abundant and never-ending stream of well-being.

From the inside out –

In this second part, you are to become the sun. You have the same power to "give" love. Remember, just like the sun, you are, and have always been, a never-ending source of energy and love (this is who you truly are). You **do not need anything in return to feel love or to radiate love.** This is your true power and nature as a human being: to expand in waves of love.

Close your eyes. And with your imagination and through your feelings, sense waves of love coming from the inside of you, and going out into the Universe. This could be done by imagining/feeling beams of light or waves of heat emanating from you. Feel that you are a sun. Feel yourself emanating peace, love, and joy. Stay in this state of *being* for as long as you want.

You are a sun of love and light in this world. Everywhere you go, hold on to this idea that you are always abundantly radiating light and love. You do not need to yell it out loud, but feel this truth. You are abundant, and when you truly understand that true abundance comes from the inside, just like the sun, you will always be a limitless source of love, and the Universe has no other choice but to keep feeding your nature with more love, more abundance, and more life.

#2 Do Less; Be More

This next technique/exercise might go against everything you ever thought to be true. In the beginning, when I discovered this, I

The Magic Spark

truly didn't want to believe it to be true. It goes against everything you and I were taught, **but as you are now aware of, you and I were taught to live life from "The Program," not from the truth of our Divine Self.** I can now tell you that if there's one technique that I go to whenever I face something difficult, or if I simply want to strengthen my faith muscles, I use this one.

Please do not underestimate the power of doing nothing. Let me explain...

When I say doing *nothing*, I am talking about the **outside world.** You and I were brought up to believe—it is ingrained in us through "The Program"—that we have to be doing stuff in order to succeed, and that the more we do, the more *chances* we have to be successful and happy. But as a matter of fact, it is the total opposite: The less you do (outside), the more you achieve.

Sorry, I guess you are *doing* something, but the *doing* is happening *inside*. Actually, you are not really ***doing***; rather, you are ***being***.

As I previously mentioned in this book, I have become very open to exploring and studying ancient wisdom, wisdom literature, spiritual practices, etc.—essentially anything that can fall into my lap—which could help me find my path to living my best life possible. I have become a student of happiness, love, joy, and peace.

In this case, I will present to you a small sentence from the Bible. I am not presenting this information to you because I want to change anything about you. My material is rated RR (religiously respectful). Whatever your spiritual practices are, I embrace you with love and respect. My intention is to show you how powerful our search for love can be, when we are open to studying the truth about love.

This quote, from the book of Psalm, has changed my life...

> ***"Be still, and know that I am God."***
> **– Psalm 46:10**

I must admit something to you. Before I ever became open to happiness (as happiness is a state of being that you must allow; as is the same with love, joy, and peace), I didn't understand what this phrase meant. In the past, I've looked at this phrase and thought that what this phrase meant was that I needed to bow in reverence to someone up in the sky. I thought I was expected to pay tribute to a deity. Today, I can tell you that for me, this is not what this means. Today, I see an incredible truth and mind-blowing message that has changed my life forever.

If it is helpful to you (and it was definitely helpful to me), I want to show you how adding simple punctuation can change the whole perspective with which you see this phrase. Right now, this sentence reads:

"Be still, and know that I am God."

But let's add some punctuation to better understand the power of what's written:

"Be still, and know that: "I am God."

IT'S A MEDITATION!

This sentence, from the book of Psalm, is a meditation! And this meditation has changed my life. My hope is that you are open to receiving this message of love. And that you understand that even in the Bible, it is written that to find the answers, to change your reality, you simply must be still **(close your eyes)** and know that you are God **(identify with the invisible part of you that is pure love—that part of you that is life itself)**.

Be still, and know that: "I am God" Meditation –

Sit in a quiet place, with soft music (no lyrics).

Start to run through your mind the fact that you came from the same Divine Intelligence that created all life. Feel how within you lies a Source Energy that you share with the trees, the sun, the oceans, and every animal and person in this life. This is how we are all connected, through one giant Source Energy—God Force—that gave us life and keeps us alive.

Once that thought has settled in, now feel that thought. Move that thought from your head into your heart. With your awareness (your noticing), try to feel this energy that is in everything.

Lastly, and the most important step of this meditation, place your attention inside of your body. Feel "*Life*" inside of you. This might feel to you like a tingly sensation inside your body; perhaps you feel some heat inside of you as you place your attention inside your body, or you feel quietness, or perhaps you might feel your heartbeat. They are all signs that you are doing this correctly. Remember, you must get rid of your analytical part. Spiritual concepts are not reasoned; they are felt. Your brain is an analytical instrument that cannot comprehend unlimited concepts. They must be felt.

As you are feeling this invisible part of you that lives inside, please remember that this part of you has no name—it is nothingness in you; it is consciousness; it is spirit; it is soul. Think of your awareness as feelings of love, peace, and abundance, as you feel this energy within.

You do not have to do much; simply feel how powerful that Divine Energy inside of you is: That is the Universe in you; that is love in you; that is the Divine Intelligence in you; that is your God Force.

From a rational perspective (your analytical brain), you might think that you are doing nothing, and that you are wasting time, and you might ask yourself: "How is this going to help me in any way with any of my problems?" That voice is your ego, the part of you that always sabotages you. **Please do not listen to that voice.**

I want to share with you that this is how I have experienced the most miracles in my life. This is my go-to technique.

The Magic Spark

Do this for as long as you can; maybe try 5 minutes to start with. This meditation helps you identify yourself with who you truly are. By using this meditation, you are reclaiming your divine power of love, happiness, peace, joy, abundance, health, etc. It is all about feeling good; it is all about remembering...

"Be still, and know that you are Source."

#3 Mental Diet

This next concept is both "food for thought" **and** "food for your thoughts."

You might have heard that what you eat (your diet) is as important, if not more important, than the amount of exercise that you do. Let's say you spend about 1 hour at the gym, every other day; but you don't have a good diet: You eat pizza for lunch and a hamburger and fries for dinner, 3 times a week. Would you lose any weight because you are going to the gym 4 times a week? Would you see any results in your weight loss journey (considering the food that you are eating)? The answer is NO.

The food you eat is very important in the fulfillment of your fitness goal! The same applies to **feeling good both mentally and spiritually.** What you give your attention to, and what you think about during the day, is called a "mental diet."

This "mental diet" exercise you are going to do, will help you have a better understanding of why you might feel the way you feel.

7 Spiritual Practices to Reclaim Your Magic Spark

It will help you see that even though you might be doing all the right "exercises at the gym," like meditating or praying, you might not be eating the "right nutrients." Let's say you meditate or pray for 30 minutes each day, but the rest of the day you react negatively to your environment; you choose to have negative thoughts, you get angry at life, or feel injustice, etc. If this is what is happening most of your days, you are not going to be able to see any results.

The following exercise is meant to create the awareness you need in order to notice what has been going into your system (your mind). This exercise is an eye opener for most people. And even though you might think that you already are on the side of positivity, please take 5–10 minutes to be honest with yourself, and do it again. I promise you will find surprises that you were not aware of before. It happened to me. I thought my mental diet was strong, and I was humbled when I discovered that I have been "cheating on my diet" most of the time.

Please be honest with yourself. And most importantly, please do not *judge* anything that you write. This is not a right or wrong exercise. This is an empowering exercise for you to become aware of the thoughts you have, so that you can make a conscious decision of changing them. Specifically, where your attention is going...

Take out a piece of paper and divide it with a line down the middle. On one side of the line, please write headline (1), and on the other side, please write headline (2):

(1) "To what am I giving my attention to during the day?"
(2) "What am I thinking of during the day?" (What are the most

The Magic Spark

prominent thoughts that occupy your mind every day? You might be surprised, but most humans repeat the same 10 thoughts every day, over and over again.)

Please answer those 2 questions, taking as much time as you need, to be honest and accurate. Please write at least 10 things on each side. It is my hope that you get as many "aha" moments as I got. These types of exercises help you develop the awareness you must have to create a new life. Your awareness is another one of the steps in my 5-step formula on creating miracles in your life! This is how important the conversation of your awareness is!

Here are some questions that might help you trigger honesty about your mental diet. This will help you jumpstart the thought process.

(1) What are you paying attention to?

- Do you watch the news? What kind of news do you listen to or see on the TV or your phone?
- Do you read any books? What kinds of books? Books that have to do with Sci-Fi, murder-cases, or apocalyptic-postwar timelines?
- What kinds of podcasts do you listen to? Podcasts about murders? Or about the end of the world?
- Do you watch Netflix? What kinds of shows do you watch? How do they make you feel (tense, anxious, and stressed (thrillers)? Are they about murders, killings, viruses, deaths, etc.?
- How long are you spending endlessly scrolling through social

media on your phone?
- What kinds of posts are you reading? Are the posts you look at motivational? Or are they mostly bad news, gossip, or mindless memes?

2) What are you thinking of?

- How often do you think about work? How does it make you feel?
- Are you thinking about that social media post that made you angry?
- Do you think about money? Do you think about money problems?
- Are you thinking about what could happen to you if…? (If you are stressing about something, it means you are not in the present; you are in the future—come back to the present.)

These are just a few lines to help you become aware of your mental diet.

After you are done with your list, please look at it and analyze it. Become the observer of the list. **Do not judge it**; simply look at it. That list, if answered honestly, will give you an accurate representation of how you feel most of the time. The most exciting thing is that you can change it.

On a separate piece of paper, please write the types of things you think the best version of you (the "you" that feels joy, happiness, peace, and love all the time) might be paying attention to and thinking of. Write the same two headlines, divided by a line down the middle, and write down, to the best of your ability, the types of things this peaceful, happy individual would be (1) paying attention to, and (2) thinking of.

Here are a few examples to help spark your creativity, but please make this your list, not mine:

(1) What are you paying attention to?

The sunrise; nature; my heartbeat; being grateful for every meal I have; how beautiful everyone is; the beauty of life; the miracle of the fact that I do not have to do anything for my body to do what it does; books on spirituality or personal development; shows that make me laugh, or shows where I learn something new; podcasts that nurture my mind and soul.

2) What are you thinking of?

Your loved ones? Your Dream Life? Your dreams? Your hobbies? Dancing? Music? How grateful you are to be alive? How grateful you are to be safe at home? How grateful you are to live in this beautiful country? How grateful you are for being you?

"What you think, you become.
What you feel, you attract.
What you imagine, you create."
– Buddha

#4 Listening to the Silence in You

"Silence is the language of God; all else is poor translation."
– Rumi

Silence will bring you peace. Please know this: *Thinking* is the cause of all turmoil in your life. The more you think about the material, rushed world, or about the things you think you *need or should* do, the more stress, anger, and unbalanced emotions you will experience. So, what's the answer? Silence.

Silence is God. Silence is Source. Meaning: Silence = Source

(Please remember that when I say the word "God" or "Source," I am referring to the Divine Intelligence that created and creates everything. It lives in you, in me, and in everything in this physical Universe.)

The reason that silence equals God or Source, is that before any creation, there is silence. Before there is sound, there is silence. Before a baby cries, there is silence. Before an idea comes into your head, there is silence. Before you were born, there was silence. Before the Big Bang, there was silence. So, in silence, you find creation. In silence, you find love. In silence, you find answers. In silence, you are not alone.

It happened to me, and it might have happened to you: In the beginning, I didn't know what to do in silence. It felt scary to simply sit alone in silence with my eyes closed. I felt afraid, simply because I was not used to it. You and I were never taught some of the most important things in life, and sitting in silence is one of them. So, don't worry; I am here to share with you that it is OK to sit in silence and do nothing. It is OK to close your eyes and be silent. It is one of the most healing practices you can have.

What to do when in silence –

It is OK if you would like to put on some background music. (Don't worry; you will still achieve silence.) Preferably, you want to choose music where there are no lyrics to the song (no one is singing, as this could be distracting), and where there is not necessarily a rhythm to the song (so you are not distracted by wanting to move). A good example is soft, classical music, and/or theta waves or any meditative, soft, and soothing music. With time, you should allow yourself the opportunity to practice this without music from time to time.

Take a deep breath. Close your eyes. Take another couple of deep breaths. And listen to your nothingness.

If your mind starts to think about anything, don't worry; make the effort and practice your awareness by noticing that you are thinking about something and not of silence. Take a deep breath and **focus again on silence.**

Here are some tools that can help you stay focused on silence:

- Listen to your heartbeat (you truly can with practice).
- Listen to silence. (This phrase makes sense in your heart; do not try to analyze it with your brain. Simply feel this phrase.)

- Say the word "ahhhhh" to yourself as you exhale (nothing loud; very softly).
- Relax your body.
- Feel the energy layer that sits outside and all around your body. (This phrase makes sense in your heart; do not try to analyze it with your brain. Simply feel this phrase.)
- Allow yourself to be free. (This phrase makes sense in your heart; do not try to analyze it with your brain. Simply feel this phrase.)

The more you practice *feeling silence,* the more you will be able to stop your thinking. On a vibrational level, you are sending a vibration of love, calmness, and peace, so the Universe has no choice but to match your vibration and send you people, circumstances, and situations to perpetuate this state of bliss. When you sit in silence, you identify yourself with your Source; you go back to being Source.

#5 Seeing Miracles

About a couple of years ago, I was in Mexico visiting some relatives. We went to a small town called Bernal. It is a hidden gem in Mexico. It is a town underneath a deserted mountain—a magical small town.

After hiking up the mountain, my family and I decided to sit down in a restaurant with a beautiful mountain view. In the middle of the restaurant, there was a 600-year-old tree! All the tables were positioned around this beautiful old tree. As we were about to eat our meals, two little boys, probably 8 and 10 years old, came into the restaurant. They were wearing Mexican sombreros, and they had a speaker with them. They began to play background music through the speaker, and they began to sing typical Mexican music. Their voices were beautiful and quite angelic.

All of a sudden, I started to tear up. Not only one but several tears came down my cheeks. My cousin looked at me and asked me what was happening. I then said: "Do you want me to tell you what I see?" Then I responded:

"Six hundred years ago, someone planted this tree in this part of the planet. As years passed, a bunch of people decided to build a town on the outskirts of this mountain that has been here for thousands of years. People lived their lives and moved on as they passed away. These two little boys were born in this little town, about 20 years after I was born, and their parents would have had to meet in a magical way for them to get married and give birth to these beautiful two souls. All of that had happened so that today, I could be here with my family, enjoying this beautiful day, in this beautiful restaurant, in this beautiful exact moment…"

Nothing happens by chance. Everything is a beautiful, orchestrated, magical piece of art. When you are able to open your perspective (see beyond what's in front of you), and you are able to start to perceive everything that has to happen for you to be enjoying any given moment in time, you realize that every second of your life is a miracle.

So this next technique is precisely that. Stop everything you are doing, as often as you can, and look around and start noticing (by opening your perspective) everything that needed to happen for you to be wherever you find yourself to be.

My wife and I had started, not so long ago, to do something very simple before every meal. It is our version of being thankful for what we are about to eat. The way we do it is a little different. It is basically applying this technique. With all my love, I share this with you so that you can start practicing the power of what I call "Seeing Beyond."

Before every meal (it doesn't matter where you are) –

Before we take the first bite, we both look at our plate of food. We close our eyes and imagine everything that needed to happen for this plate of food to be right in front of us: the farmer who raised the vegetables with his hard work and love; the vegetables, which out of small seeds grew into something as time passed by; the people that transported the vegetables from the farm into the stores, and how they do that job (transportation) to feed their own families; the fish that gave its life for us to have this dinner tonight; the person that keeps the grocery store clean and organized; the people that trust my wife and I with our skills, in exchange for a salary, etc. All of that and more, for her and I to be enjoying this beautiful, nutritious plate of food, right here, right now… And by the time we are about to finish our visualization, we look at each other as we acknowledge how lucky we are to be in each other's company, and all the miracles that needed to happen for us to be sitting together, wherever we are, with us, right now…

As you practice this "Seeing Beyond" technique, you are understanding from your heart how connected we all are. You are allowing yourself to realize how blessed you are, and how this God Force (the Universe) moves literally *everything* in this planet just for you. You are growing your miracle muscles. You are expanding your sense of gratitude. And the more you do this, the more you create the habit of peace.

Please remember:
"It's not what you look at; it's what you see."

#6 Stop Feeding the Fire

You are about to read one of the most powerful techniques you could ever practice in your life. This next technique is one of the most incredible tools I have ever put into practice for letting go of any negative feeling in my body. In the past, I've always asked myself: "What does it mean to let go? How do you even let go?" The following is the closest I've ever gotten to understanding what that truly means.

It is quite obvious, but if you were to create a bonfire, as soon as you stop putting wood into the fire, the fire has no other option but to eventually run out of "fuel," and it will cease to exist; the fire will extinguish. The same goes for any negative or painful feeling that might have come into your life experience due to an undesired experience.

This is the exact technique I used to let go of the feelings of fear, anxiety, and stress that flared up when I lost my job when the pandemic happened. This is the technique you can apply to *anything* you might be going through.

Our minds are trained to "fuel the fire," but what does this mean? As soon as something "negative" happens in our lives and we feel negative emotions as a result of that experience, you and I start spiraling. In my case, as soon as I got the phone call from the company, to let me know they were doing some lay-offs, and that I was part of that group, my mind started spiraling into other thoughts. I first thought, "How am I going to pay my bills?" **(This right here was adding a log to the "fire.")** Then other thoughts started to invade my head: "My savings are not enough to sustain my family for long" **(this here was adding another log to the "fire")**; "No one is hiring right now" **(this here was adding yet another log to the "fire")**; "I cannot survive if this keeps going on for long" **(this here was adding yet another log to the "fire")**; "I am not good enough, and that's why they let me go and not someone else" **(this here was adding yet another log to the "fire")**; and so on... you get the idea.

Every thought you add to any "negative" experience in your head, is "adding a log to the fire." By the end of your spiraling, the "fire" will be so big and "fueled up" that it will result in a panic attack. Not only that, but at the same time, you are giving your attention (your God Force) to thoughts and feelings that are making you feel really bad; therefore, you will only attract into your life experience more of those same emotions and feelings. The question here is: "How do I let go of all of that? How do I *heal* from what has happened?"

The most interesting thing is that most of the thoughts that you even spiral into are either not true or don't ever come true.

Stop Feeding the Fire –

This technique is a 4-step technique:

Identify the feeling you want to let go:

You must identify the feeling underneath **what happened.** Whoever or whatever causes you to feel a certain way is not what you are going to focus on… You are going to focus on the feeling that you feel, not on the cause. Please be very precise with identifying what you feel: Is it anger, frustration, anxiety, pain, envy, stress, etc.? What is the feeling that you are feeling?

Stop judging and/or condemning yourself for having the feeling:

You might judge yourself or continuously ask yourself, "Why am I feeling this?" Or you might simply tell yourself that "it is not correct to feel this way," or "I shouldn't feel this way." PLEASE **STOP**. You feel the way you feel—period. Stop accumulating more judgmental thoughts that are useless to have (stop feeding the fire). Do not judge yourself for feeling what you feel.

Stop feeding the fire:

This is an extremely important step. **Do not think of any thought linked to the circumstance or person that caused you to feel the way you feel.** Do not "spiral down" into multiple thoughts that then make you spiral into more negative thoughts. If you catch yourself *spiraling*, take a deep breath and come back to the present moment, and come back to the original **feeling**, the one you have identified that you are going to let go.

Stay with the feeling of what happened. Simply feel the feeling. Perhaps it is fear; perhaps it is anxiety, or perhaps it is stress. Identify what you are feeling, and stop thinking about what caused it. At the end of the day, what happened is not important; what's important is what you feel (your reaction) toward what happened.

Sit in silence with the original feeling:

This right here might be the most important step of them all. You might not feel comfortable at first, but this is how to "let go." Close your eyes and feel the feeling, the one feeling that you have identified as painful.

Think about a pressure cooker. The pressure needs to come out; otherwise, it would explode. This is what you are doing, in a spiritual sense, to your body and to yourself. You are allowing the pain to leave your body. You are allowing the pressure of the inside to simply be. Do not be afraid. Sit with the feeling. Do not force it out; and remember, **do not dwell on what happened, and do not think/add any other additional thought to what happened.**

The Magic Spark

Simply sit there and allow the feeling to be felt. The more you learn how to do this, without judging what you are feeling, and without adding more negative thoughts to your original feeling, the more you will let go.

It might seem scary at first, as you and I were never taught to face our emotions. But I promise you that it might take a few minutes, or it might take a few days, but if you apply this technique under these four steps, you will learn how to let go. You will feel liberated. You will start to climb up through the levels of consciousness. You will be able to start accessing better feeling emotions. This is your way back to peace.

This technique can be applied to anything that has ever happened to you in the past: a break-up, losing something or someone, betrayal, a disappointment, etc. You and I are energy beings, and we are not supposed to hold on to anything (not even positive energy). Energy should flow through us (energy never stops moving). We allow positive energy to flow through us; we feel it and we let it go, but we tend to keep negative emotions inside. We tend to hold on to negative feelings. This technique will help you go back to your natural state of being; it will help you let go of what has been stuck.

You can apply this technique one negative feeling at a time. Identify one negative feeling that has been stuck in your body (and in your mind) for a while. Apply the "stop feeding the fire" technique, by allowing yourself to feel that feeling and not give it any power whatsoever (as described in the steps above). When you are done releasing the pressure on that particular feeling (you will know when), you can move on to a different negative or stuck emotion. Always remember to be kind, patient, and unconditionally loving to yourself. You are now learning how to use your body, mind, and spirit. You are learning new things about yourself. In the beginning, it will take exploration and practice, just like when you were learning to ride a bike or when you were learning how to draw. It is quite exciting to know that there is so much more to learn, especially when it comes to living your Dream Life.

#7 Your True Identity

As you previously read in Chapter 4 (The 5 Things You've Forgotten About Your Magic Spark), the ego is an artificial intelligence created by you (unconsciously). The ego, the *false self,* thrives when it perceives separation and desperation. So, in order for the ego to survive, it clings to your identity (your name, age, gender, nationality, job title, etc.), because the more you identify yourself with any of these labels, the more the ego will push you to believe that you are separate from everyone and everything else. Ego will push you to feel like you are living in a "me vs. them" situation. Your ego will always push you to judge and categorize yourself and others through false descriptors, such as good, bad, tall, short, fat, skinny, smart, stupid, ugly, pretty, nice person, not a nice person, etc. The ego will always perpetuate separation... But remember, you are not your ego.

The following practice will help you strengthen your ability to connect with who you really are, and not with the ego (false self). It personally helped me find peace after I had lost it for quite a while. Through this practice, you are experiencing your Highest Self. And the more you practice connecting with who you truly are, the more everything around you will change, as if by magic.

Feeling your Highest Self –

Remember, as you read in Chapter 4 (The 5 Things You've Forgotten About Your Magic Spark), **you are a *loving, creative, kind, beautiful, abundant, and ever-expanding being.*** This is your true identity. These characteristics are your birthright; they cannot be taken away from you. This is **who you are**.

Find a quiet space, and perhaps put on some soothing music (no lyrics involved). You are going to close your eyes and take a couple of deep breaths.

1st part –

You are going to imagine a beautiful source of light shining outside of you. Try to feel at peace with this beautiful light and its warming nature. After you have a clear image of it, *feel* the following characteristics emanating from this beautiful source of light, and how they start to surround you. Please feel this to the best of your abilities; this is where the success of this practice lies, in imagining and feeling it. Take a couple of minutes for each one, and then move on to the next. Imagine this beautiful source of light as:

Loving – You might want to imagine how this source of light emanates love for you. Imagine the feeling of a warm, loving wave of light hugging you.

Kind – Imagine how this source of light is kind to all living things in this Universe.

Beautiful – Picture whatever comes to mind that is beautiful in this world: a beach, a sunrise, a mother with her child, a panda, your puppy, your cat, etc. Feel how beautiful it all is.

Abundant – Imagine how this source of light is abundant; it is what the sun is made of. And it never stops giving. Be in awe at how this energy never stops giving love.

Creative – Imagine how this beautiful source of light is in all living and non-living things; how it created all there is, and how it is at all times creating. Once it gives "birth" to something, it moves on from its perfect creation, to the next one. It does not create anything by accident.

Expanding – Imagine how this beautiful source of light is always growing and expanding. It has never stopped expanding. It is expanding as you read this and imagine it.

2nd part –

You are now going to imagine that these same 6 characteristics of this beautiful source **are coming from you.** The goal is for you to identify yourself with them, and feel each one of them coming from within, emanating from you. As I mentioned before, you came from this Source, this Divine Intelligence, and this is your true identity. Now it is time for you to start identifying yourself with who you truly are, and to feel who you truly are.

Loving – Imagine and feel how love is all you are. Feel that you love all there is. Imagine you are a loving machine.

Kind – Imagine yourself as being kind to others, especially to yourself. Feel it.

Beautiful – Feel how beautiful you are; how beautiful your body is, as it gives you the opportunity to have this human experience. You are beautiful!

Abundant – You are an abundant being. You are always *giving something* to this world. Repeat to yourself: "I Am Abundant," and start exploring how to feel what that means.

Creative – You are a creative being. Every second of every day, you are creating with your thoughts and feelings. Reclaim that powerful creator you are, and recognize that everything that has happened to you up to this point, you had a part in its creation. You have the ability to create anything you want. Start owning that you are the creator of your own reality. You are creative!

Expanding – Imagine yourself as an ever-expanding ball of energy. You were placed into this world to keep expanding, to evolve, to transform. Simply imagine yourself as a ball of energy that keeps growing and growing; most importantly, feel how this feels. Explore feeling the expansion of your "self."

When you finish, open your eyes and enjoy the feeling of now knowing who you are. As you continue your day, do your best to remember these 6 characteristics throughout your day, no matter what you think is happening.

This is you. This is who you are. As you are getting more familiarized with this practice, especially in the beginning, you may or may not feel these as strong; you may or may not have tears running down your cheeks (I did). Try to open your heart as much as you can. And have patience with these new things you're doing. It is all good; it is all perfect.

Living From Your Magic Spark

At the end of my books, I love bringing it all together. I am leaving you with key pointers to practice along your way. These key concepts were deeply explored in this book, but the reason for this summary, is to help you focus on practicing and feeling your Magic Spark. Please follow your heart—your Magic Spark—and practice what resonates the most with you, and what seems the most challenging to practice; there is a hidden lesson for you in there.

#1 Your Magic Spark

This is who you really are. You are the entire Universe expressed in physical form. Your Magic Spark is that formless, invisible part of you that was never born, and therefore, it can never die. It is the energy that exists everywhere; it exists in all living and non-living things. And it is the true voice of *love* that is always guiding you when you stop and listen.

#2 Your True Characteristics

Stop identifying yourself with your name, gender, nationality, job title, and age. You are far more than that. As you've learned throughout this book, you have the same characteristics as the Source you came from. You are *loving, kind, beautiful, abundant, creative, ever-expansive, reciprocal, and eternal.* Begin to describe yourself having these characteristics; this is who you really are. The more you recognize all of these true qualities in yourself, the more your life will get back to its true nature: perfect abundance.

#3 Love vs. Fear

Remember that at all times, there are always two energies inside of you. You can either choose to live from LOVE, which is the energy where you are a creator. With LOVE, you have power; things happen for you, and there is no way you can be a victim. With LOVE, you create a new life; you are in tune with your true spirit. Or you can choose to live your life from FEAR. *Fear* is the lack of love in your life. Through *fear,* you will experience a lack mentality, and you will experience life as a victim (things happen to you). Fear is just an illusion of separation—it is a lack of faith and belief in love.

Be aware of the following question at all times; it will help you know which direction or place you are choosing to live your life from (love or fear): **"What I am about to think, say, or do, will it bring me peace, or will it bring me turmoil?"**

#4 Abundance

Abundance is all there is. This concept is so key to understand. This concept alone can change your entire life. Remember, there is either abundance of abundance (meaning abundance of more), or abundance of lack (meaning abundance of less). Whichever you pay attention to, it will expand, and you will create more of the same. This Universe will never stop being abundant, so you can choose to pay attention to the fact that there is an abundance of love, or you can choose to pay attention to the fact that there is an abundance of fear—you choose!

#5 Whose Life Are You Living (Limiting Beliefs)?

This is one of the most important conversations you and I can have, and I hope you are open to it. There is a 95% chance that you are not living the life you want, and that you are living the life someone else told you that you should. Become aware of the thoughts you have toward money, religion, love, food, spirituality, success, etc.... Where do they come from? Who told you that life is supposed to be that way?

Please remember that you think you "know" how life is supposed to be, because someone else explained "life" to you. But someone else explained "life" to that person too, and so on... You have been programmed to believe things like, "You must work hard for money or success," "Too much money is evil," "There is an authority outside of you," "Asking for help is called cheating (in school)," etc. All of these are limiting beliefs that are not serving an abundant, prosperous, and joyful life.

Please know that there is only one truth: You are meant to experience love, happiness, peace, prosperity, health, and joy. You are perfect, whole, and complete. And any thought outside of this, comes from ego (a false self).

#6 Your Ego

One of the most important concepts you could ever think of, is that there are two of you inside of you. There is the **real you**—your

Divine Self, your Magic Spark—and there is your **ego**—the false self—an idea of who you and others think you are.

Living your life from ego will always cause you suffering, lack, and separation. On the contrary, living from your Magic Spark, your real self, will always connect you with your Source, and will lead you back to your natural state of being of love, happiness, peace, and joy.

Your ego is all the labels you currently identify yourself with, like your name, gender, nationality, age, and job title. You must learn how NOT to identify yourself with that which is limited and can perish (like your name, gender, nationality, age, job title, etc.), and start identifying yourself with that which is eternal, your true identity—abundance, creativity, love, and perfection. You are the entire Universe expressed in physical form.

#7 Your Purpose

By the simple fact that you showed up, you have a purpose. And by the way, we all share the same purpose: to be a loving energy to others. But how it expresses itself is what is unique to you and me.

Remember that your purpose is not something you look for out there; rather, you allow it from the inside out. Your purpose is the unique way you see life, and it must be expressed. It is the biggest gift you can give others and yourself—the unique expression of how you interpret life. Stop chasing the seeking of your purpose *out there*; simply honor and do more of what inspires you in this life.

> *"Your life is not about you. Your life is about everyone else whose life you touch and the way you touch it."*
> – Neal Donald Walsch

#8 It is all happening at the same time!

This is one of the most freeing thoughts you can understand. We tend to believe that if we are feeling stress right now, *stress* is all that is happening, but this is not true. The entire spectrum of feelings and consciousness is happening all the time. If you and I feel stress right now, there is for sure someone out there feeling peace, and/or joy, and/or love, and/or sadness, and/or anger, etc.

This means that it is up to us to use our awareness to move through the different levels of consciousness (feelings), and get out of the reality we are creating while being stuck feeling; in this case, *stress.*

It is all happening at the same time: abundance, love, happiness, peace, neutrality, fear, hatred, anger, anxiety, depression, etc. What do you choose to tune into?

> **"A change of feeling is a change of destiny"**
> **– Neville Goddard**

#9 Seeing Miracles

Miracles are happening all the time. The only way you can perceive them is by being present. The fact that you can breathe is a miracle; the fact that your heart is beating, without you doing anything, is a miracle; the fact that the sun is floating in the middle of nowhere and providing life to us, is a miracle.

Perceiving miracles is a skill that you had when you were a baby, which you started losing as you believed the things adults tend to believe in.

The more you practice seeing miracles, the more miracles you will see. It's like when you are thinking of buying a particular car in a particular color, and you start to see that car, in that color, everywhere!

Miracles are always present. Are you looking at them? Or are you looking at your past and/or future for the things that didn't work out or the things you don't want to happen?

#10 Stop Looking Outside

There is a natural feeling to always be searching for more… the reason being that we are beings of expansion. It is in our nature to keep evolving; we are unlimited… but you tend to look in the wrong places (outside). You and I have been conditioned that we must look for the evidence outside of us, and this is wrong.

When we feel stress, anxiety, fear, or depression, it is because we are searching for our answers outside of us. When we feel good, it's because we have looked in the right places (inside) and found that which we were looking for.

You can never find what you are looking for outside of you, because the *idea to look for something* in the first place, came from within; so it is only inside that you can find what you are looking for.

It is not about *wanting*; it is about *being*. To *want* is to try to pull something from the outside in, and it means that we currently do not have what we desire. By *law,* it will stay that way, as by *wanting,* we are simply saying that in this moment, we do not have it. To *be,* on the other hand, is to push from the inside out. It is recognizing that you already are that which you desire to be; therefore, the outside world must reflect that which you are already inside—this is the *Law of Expression.*

#11 Thank you for saying *"YES"* to you, by reading this book

I hope you are beginning to understand and accept the incredible and perfect being that you are.

My mission is to allow you to notice who you really are, and in a sense, help you realize and understand how powerful you are, and that you already have everything you need and ever wanted.

I am not here to "help you." Saying that I am here to help you would imply that there is something missing or wrong about you.

The Magic Spark

Let me tell you something: There is nothing wrong about you. You already are perfect, beautiful, loving, kind, creative, and abundant, exactly the way you are. You simply must notice it by closing your eyes and feeling those things from the inside out. Never wait for something on the outside to change how you feel on the inside. Humans have always practiced this formula backwards; the true way is as follows: You must feel happy, loving, healthy, and abundant first, in order for your happiness, self-love, healing, and prosperity to show up in your life.

A great British writer, named Alan Watts, had this beautiful analogy, which I would love to close this book with. I will take his initial concept and express it in my own words.

#12 It Was a MUSICAL Thing

We tend to think that life is a journey; we've heard this so many times. But saying that life is a journey implies that there is a beginning and an end; it implies that some kind of *traveling from one place to another* needs to happen. And if it was up to you and me, we would skip the *traveling* part. We would simply want to get to the destination as fast as we could.

Music, on the other hand, is playful by nature. You never say: **"I am going to *work* the piano."** You say, "I am going to *play* the piano." When you are listening to your favorite song, you do not want it to end; you enjoy the beginning, the middle, and the end. You enjoy the high notes as much as the low notes. You don't rush to the end of the song… Or if you go to a concert, you don't go to simply listen to the last 5 seconds of the last song; you enjoy the entire experience. Otherwise, the best concerts would be the ones where the musician plays the fastest so that he/she can get to the end.

When you dance, for example, you allow your body to feel the music. You are not really aiming at a particular spot on the dance floor; you simply flow with the song as it is being played along the way, and your body moves with the music, not knowing what the next movement will be.

This is why we got this whole *life* thing all wrong. It is not a journey; it is a *musical* thing. And you are supposed to sing, you are supposed to play, you are supposed to dance, you are supposed to be happy… while the music is still playing.

"You are a piece of the master. You are a masterpiece."
– **Les Brown**

About the Author

Rodrigo Diaz Mercado lives in Toronto, Canada.

The author is available for on-site and online lectures and workshops, keynote presentations, speaking events, personal consulting, conferences, seminars, and individual training to appropriate audiences (large and small) around the world.

Rodrigo has worked with organizations, businesses, corporations, and universities and colleges interested in helping their staff, colleagues, and students to boost their happiness, mental and emotional health, innovation, productivity, creativity, and more—all through using neuroscientific and mindful principles and practices. For more information about Rodrigo and his conferences, please visit:

HappyLivingInstitute.com

Help Rodrigo Díaz Mercado to spread this message of empowerment and understanding to everyone around you. For rates and availability, please contact the author directly, at:

rodrigodiazmercado@gmail.com

You can also contact Rodrigo for personalized coaching sessions that will help you build a map to live the life of your dreams, and create REAL MAGIC in your life. In these sessions, you can leave behind a past that does not work, and you can focus on the present, to live the desires and achieve the goals you want by increasing your emotional and spiritual intelligence. For rates and availability, please contact the author directly, at:

rodrigodiazmercado@gmail.com

Rodrigo has created an online course just for you: Creating Magic in Your Life. In this course, you will learn and practice the habits of creating magic in your life; you will understand how to attract the life of your dreams, and how to create the habits of love, peace, joy, and happiness. To join the online course, and learn more details about it, please go to:

HappyLivingInstitute.com/courses

To order more books, or to get Rodrigo's first book, *Sleight of Mind – How to Create & Experience Magic in Your Life*, please contact the author directly, visit Amazon.com, or visit:

HappyLivingInstitute.com/books

You can also get Rodrigo's FREE eBook, *How to Create a New Personal Reality*, by visiting:

HappyLivingInstitute.com/ebook

Connect with Rodrigo through social media!
Facebook and LinkedIn: Rodrigo Diaz Mercado
Instagram: Sleight_of_Mind

About the Author

Finally, if you have been inspired by this book, the best thing you could ever do is pass it on and be a wonderful role model for others. This world needs more magic; this world needs more of your magic.

www.ingramcontent.com/pod-product-compliance
Lightning Source LLC
Chambersburg PA
CBHW070533170426
43200CB00011B/2414